Counting Bones

Dear Darla,

This is the book I'd told you about (did you go on her website?) I finally read this on our way to Elmira. It certainly was enlightening for me! Am hoping her story and recovery will help you, too.

Love,
Faye

Counting Bones

Michelle J. Bahret

Milo House Press
New York, New York

Copyright © 2002 Counting Bones, Michelle J. Bahret, All right reserved.

ISBN: 1-59268-017-8

Milo House Press
New York, New York

GMAPublishing@aol.com
GMAPublishing.com

All rights reserved. No portion of this book may be reproduced, stored in a retrieval system, or transmitted in any form or by any other means- electronic, mechanical, photocopy, recording or any other except for brief quotations in printed reviews, without the prior permission of the publisher.

Cover By: Rhonda Hodge
Cover Photo: Linda Tillson
Manuscript Assistant: John Beanblossom

Printed in the United States of America

Table of Contents:

Introduction		1
Part I	The Illness	4
Part II	The Transition	135
Part III	The Complete Surrender	172
Epilogue		203

Introduction

Dear Reader,

You are about to an encounter an intimate experience of what it's like to live inside the head of a young woman suffering with an eating disorder. I am inviting you to read a series of journal entries that I kept during an often-pendulous swing of illness, hope, recovery, back to the pit of despair, and ultimate triumph. Although I have a 15 year history of struggling with anorexia and bulimia, I chose only to include entries from 1995 to the current year 2001 as these latter years were the most poignant, and which I learned and resurrected from, the most.

I first had the idea to transform my entries into published format in 1999 after watching an Oprah Winfrey talk show on eating disorders. Oprah asked this question, which seems to resonate with thousands of people, "What is going on inside her head?" It occurred to me that I could help answer this question by allowing people to read inside my own inner dialogue recorded in my journals. They are my thoughts that I had in the height of my illness and my struggle to free myself from its tenacious grasp. Of course, at the time, I had no idea that it might be open for other eyes to see. I did not have that mindset; all I was trying to do was to hold on until I could find a way out, and writing was a mode of escape. I also wrote because I couldn't find my voice. Now, I hope my writing can be a voice to others going through this experience and for desperate family members and friends who don't know what to say or do to help.

There are some factors to keep in mind while reading this book. Ultimately, this is a story of my salvation and redemption through my Lord, Jesus Christ. However, two-thirds of this book is not very Christian-like. It will be uncomfortable at times to read, maybe even offensive, but it's important to me to tell my story as it happened. I sincerely believe that if I were to alter it in any way that I would be taking glory away from God. As you read, please keep in mind that there are beliefs or ideas I once had that are no longer truthful for me. The whole story in context will reveal this transformation. Moreover, there is sensitive material regarding family relationships. What I have written is through my perspective and what I was feeling at the time. Although I do not blame my family whatsoever, having an eating disorder is not just the individual's problem, but the family's as well. It would be impossible to tell my story without referring to them in some way. Happily, our situation is not as it once was, but I do hope that this would be enlightening and healing for everyone involved.

Today I am healthy (praise God) but for many years I was quite ill and I didn't have a personal relationship with God. My thoughts and ideas were very much based upon worldly philosophies. I didn't know the Word of God and, therefore, had little knowledge about spiritual warfare or the weapon to fight against it. Yet, you will see I was desperate for God. I was always crying out to him. At one point, I write, "I feel like I need a spiritual guide". I didn't know it then, but that person's name is Jesus!

The structure of this book is divided into three sections. The first, and longest, deals with the illness and mindset of the eating disorder. The second section includes my Christian adoption and tentative steps forging into recovery. The third section reveals my complete surrender to Christ after a devastating relapse. It confirms just how fast God can work through our lives when we allow him to! I believe I went through what I did, for as long as I did, so that I would become a living testimony of God's power, mercy, and enduring love. How could I keep this to myself? And when I have struggled with doubt and fear about proceeding with my story, God led me to this scripture:

Mark 4:21-29

He said to them, "Do you bring in a lamp to put it under a bowl or a bed? Instead, don't you put it on its stand? For whatever is hidden is meant to be disclosed, and whatever is concealed is meant to be brought out into the open. If anyone has ears to hear, let him hear."

He also said, "This is what the kingdom of God is like. A

Counting Bones

man scatters seed on the ground. Night and day, whether he sleeps or gets up, the seed sprouts and grows, though he does not know how. All by itself the soil produces grain- first the stalk, then the head, then the full kernel in the head. As soon as the grain is ripe, he puts the sickle to it, because the harvest has come."

These scriptures helped me to acknowledge that God is in control, in charge of this whole process, and if anyone needs to hear my story, who am I to withhold the miracle God has worked in my life? If one person can hear let them hear...nothing could make me happier to know that I helped one person. I am always mindful that it is God and not my own will that has led me to this place. Now, I will let the story unfold and speak for itself...

Michelle Bahret
August 2001

Part I

The ILLNESS

On faith and gratitude:

Happy New Year!
1/1/95
God promises us blessings and great abundance. We are blessed. We are children of God. By learning to see the many blessings and graciousness of God, we become more gracious to other people. Sometimes it is hard to see the work of God in everyday life. Our pain, anxiety, and frustration get in the way. However, by taking time out each day before going to bed and reflecting what we're thankful for that day, it becomes easier to see. We begin to see more and more the blessings and promise of abundance. By building our gratitude over negative thinking, we become more in tune to these blessings, and the more in tune we are, the easier it is to rely on them during troubling, uncertain times. We become more loving and forgiving; more gracious. By being thankful for each day at a time, it is not overwhelming as trying to produce a major overhaul of bad habits. So this first day of the New Year, I'm really thankful for the people I was with; that I wasn't alone. I had fun. And I'm thankful that I made it to this day.

On handling conflict:
1/10/95
I realized, for myself, to discuss my conflicts out loud. To hear myself out loud helps me to feel calmer inside. I feel peaceful when I recognize what I'm saying. Indeed, my voice is more rational than my head. There's a tape that plays in my head, but when I speak, it breaks that pattern.

On family dynamics:
Complicated issues arise by having developed beyond the family in every area. I grew up observing which allowed me to get

smart. I didn't interact much because I already wasn't functioning at their level. There were things I recognized as dysfunctional. Now, I don't fit in, but my eating disorder allows me to be dysfunctional. The most difficult lesson is recognizing that I don't fit in and accepting it.

On becoming a Movie Star:
1/17/95
When they ask what I'm doing, they're really not thinking that much into it. They expect me to be in California because that's where the entertainment is but I don't think they realize what it takes. All they're thinking is that I'm someone they will know. Not many people usually carry out what I'm planning to do. It's the same as saying, "I want to be an astronaut." It's very unusual and very difficult. What I want to do is exciting. People who are in entertainment are out of context with our world. We're used to seeing these people inside our boxes. Seeing the real, breathing person is unreal.

College Graduation Night:
1/28/95
What a wonderful, wonderful evening. Graduation was beautiful. I felt so happy. It was so exciting to walk across the stage and accept my diploma. It's really a miracle.

On Body Image:
1/31/95
In therapy, I talked about my distortions. Even if I were to eat an entire day non-stop, it would be impossible for me to become fat. It's an illogical fear. I'm afraid of out-of-control eating but I have the body type where I can pretty much eat what I want and maintain my weight. Additionally, talked about the "princess" label I seem to have unwillingly adopted in this family. The feeling seems to be that I'm a spoiled princess who receives everything on a silver platter. "Welcome to the real world" is a real discount of my achievements. The deepest level is that they all feel guilty because they know they have left me holding the bag. They don't understand all of this on a conscious level of course, but it's important that I understand it. It's important for me to remember

that even when I feel like Jell-O inside, I am a strong and tenacious person.

2/7/95
In therapy, I addressed my phobic fear of being rejected by family if I don't succeed in my professional endeavors. My fear is that I'm not going to be able to handle that kind of pain and the pain I'm suffering now is more bearable. At a time when things are more uncertain as ever, my eating disorder is familiar. I know how to do it and do it well. Each time I fall back is for a different reason, but the familiarity draws me to it.

2/16/95
I'm finding when I surround myself with caring, supportive people; it's easier to take care of myself. However, after the weekend, I took two steps backward. I started throwing up again and cutting back on meals. The feeling was, "I don't know if I like this, so I'm going to stick to what I know best."

In Peer Ministry we talked about conformity and daring to be different. What's the one trait or value that we'd defend even in the face of consternation? I expressed, "I y'am who I y'am" (derived from "Popeye"). I dare to speak the truth and I have courage to be who I am.

On Self-Realization:
2/24/95
I realized that if you are given a gift from God, the worst thing that you can do is deny it. If this is my calling from God, I owe it to him to answer it.
(Prior to auditioning for the Academy Of Musical and Dramatic Arts in New York City)

3/4/95
Today's homily was on temptation. Jesus was tempted by the devil. It described how Satan did most of the talking, and God remained quiet. By keeping quiet, that is how he won the battle. Temptation speaks louder. God's voice is just a little whisper.

3/6/95
    I don't need to gratify my ego every time it gets stepped on.

3/21/95
    In session, talked about how I felt my birthday was a miracle. It's the first time I have wanted to be alive.

4/3/95
    My friend Amy paid me the greatest compliment by saying I looked at peace. She said she had liked me right away because I was real.

On the Inner Child:
5/2/95
    One way I could help myself is to embrace the little girl in me. I need to have more fun, be more playful and creative. I should color, play with clay, build sandcastles at the beach, eat cotton candy, etc. It's the most wondrous feeling to look at the stars or sit on the beach at twilight.
    When I don't eat, I'm not living. I'm afraid to live, I'm afraid to feel good. It's hard to laugh and share time with people. It's hard to choose life over death and light over darkness. But I have to trust in God and in myself that this darkness will pass.

5/4/95
    I have a confusion that success=smaller. And when I feel abandoned, misunderstood, and not listened to, I react by getting skinnier.

On outside perception:
6/4/95
    I was so flattered when one of the residents at work told me she could learn a lot from me. She said I seemed very smart and intelligent. When I asked her how she came to this conclusion, she said it was how I carried myself and held a conversation. She wanted to know what "normal" was. I asked, "What's normal?" and she replied, "you."

My own perception:
6/13/95

I've been at both ends of the spectrum. When I was near normal weight, I had more energy, improved coloring, and didn't think about food as much. Juxtapose that experience with my experience of being underweight and the evidence is there for me to see. It's the hardest thing to accept.

Identifying a "trigger" that caused a relapse:
6/27/95

When I looked at pictures of myself, I saw a healthy, normal person but I still felt traumatized inside, so I lost all the weight. I keep thinking that I'm fat regardless of what I weigh because I want to do away with my body. If I have no body, there's nothing to molest. I thought that the smaller I got, I could hide in a small corner, and therefore, not be found.

7/5/95

Doubt, fear, and insecurity. Those are my three demons.

7/21/95

It's as if this disease is like a demon possessing my body. The "good" voices are all the people telling me the truth; that I'm too thin, I'm not eating, and I'm worth something. The "evil" voice is the one telling me not to believe it. I have to throw up. I'm not emaciated. How can they say I am? I tune out all the good voices. The evil voice is like a magnet; it captures all my attention. Even when I want to look away; it rails me in, hook, line, and sinker.

On the pace of recovery:
7/24/95

It's not the mountain's top that's important so much as the mountain climbing. I'm trying to find myself when I've been here all along! It's more about finding peace and a fulfilled life. I'm a human being, not a human doing.

On God:

There was no one like me before I came into this world nor will there be after I leave. I make people's lives different with my presence. Feeling "not quite right" is a perfectionism issue. Everyone has a piece missing.

7/27/95
Marilyn: A friend's commentary:
   She says my writing reflects the core of my being. When she reads my letters, it's as if I'm in the room with her. My writing reflects how I would say it if I were talking.

On dreams and aspirations:
8/2/95
   I just see myself as a little wrapped package and inside is a blockbuster talent. Only I have to untie the bow! I'm wasting my talent by not exploring it.

On making the decision to terminate therapy:
8/3/95
   I know myself well enough to handle conflict. I know my issues. I've learned all the tools and how to use them. I have wonderful people around me who will keep me up. I think it's a good thing to move beyond therapy and try other things. I need to challenge my growth.

On the mother/daughter struggle:
8/7/95
   I had a right to be taken care of with no strings attached. But the feeling was, "I'll give you food and shelter, but you have to be grateful for it." She's holding the end of the rope. A child shouldn't feel it's a privilege to be taken care of.
   Now it's difficult to take care of myself. By controlling my food intake, I'm saying, "you can't take this away from me." I have the rope in my hands. I've got the power but it's not empowerment.

A colleague's commentary:
8/8/95
   I'm described as someone "not backing down", that I am a person who can hold her own.

Michelle Bahret

On Prayer:
   Praying to God is like calling a friend. Sometimes there's a busy signal, and you can't get through. So, you try again. If you don't, you make no contact.
You might not get instant answers. What may be the right answer for you may not be the same plan God has in mind. Success may be so gradual you don't realize you're making progress until someone comments on how "together" you are or at peace. Or maybe you just start feeling better. But one thing is sure, if you give up; you'll never get through.

8/11/95
   I see a pattern of the "old" blending with the "new". Even though I'm taking steps forward, the old behaviors seem to keep up with me. With this new sense of budding confidence and freedom, is a rising fear that surrounds my weight, body image, but most importantly my role in the world and the people around me. I have an unrealistic view of whom I am and what I have to offer. Sometimes I can see that eating more is not losing control but gaining control. The obsession with my weight keeps me distracted from real-life issues. It inhibits everything I have to give. It keeps me small, vulnerable, and weak. I think I even underestimate the power and strength I have to overcome this foe. That this way of life is not something I need to settle for. I can overcome it. It is simple but just as complicated, as giving myself permission to be free. However, at the same time, nothing can still the panic the moment the numbers fluctuate on the scale. With all my knowledge and understanding, I don't know what it takes to jump this last hurdle. I suppose, as with everything else, it's just trusting in God. It's so hard.

On Self-affirmation:
   If anyone is talking to me disrespectfully, I have the right to tell him or her not to, even if it's Mom. It doesn't matter that she pays the bills. That is irrelevant. My self-worth is not attached to material things that she gives to me.
   There is a difference between selfishness and self-care. Much of it has to do with instinct. Does this feel right? What other people think is good for me, may not be. That's hard. That's

when I need to stand up for myself.

Validating my feelings is self-care. Meeting my own needs is self-care. Whatever I do that is considered selfish is only in the eye of the beholder. I don't need anyone's approval but my own. I haven't given that to my Self.

Self-care means not hurting myself, i.e., not eating or getting sick. Having an eating disorder does not make me a bad person. So often, morality is applied to eating disorders; that because I do this to myself, then it is my fault for being sick. I'm weak. But I didn't choose this. No one in their right mind would ever choose this.

I struggle with the Catholic belief that suicide is a sin. God doesn't just look at the cause of death: she died from anorexia, she gets the boot! He considers the whole story.

I've been pondering the nature of my illness. Is it like alcoholism or can there be a 100% recovery? Is it like a waterfall, which shoots straight down to the goal? Or is it a river that winds around, up and down? Or is it like an ocean that ebbs in and out? Sometimes it seems like a combination. Right now it feels like two steps forward and two steps back. I think it's mostly like a river but I think family expects it to be like a waterfall. I think my problem (with family), is that I speak the truth and confront issues.

On Sibling Roles and "Rivalry":
8/22/95

Skeletons and secrets revealed during a dinner invite from Kevin and Chrissy. Somehow the past came up in discussion and there were heated emotions. Among the topics were racism and adultery. Kevin hadn't known about Granddad's affair, whose unfaithfulness was inherited by Dad. I could relate to Kevin's anger in response to Dad's lack of support but Kathy thought he was just being stubborn and pig-headed like the old block.

Kathy is limited in how much she can look at and deal with. Everything came to a "screeching halt" when her brain went into over-load and she couldn't hear anymore. Of course, I had to leave with her since she was my ride home. I was so mad because I wanted to keep talking. For the first in a long time, I felt like I was getting my own say. It felt healthy to be getting all this crap out in the open. All of a sudden she decides she's leaving and asked if I were coming and I said, "I don't have a choice". Kevin and Chrissy both laughed uncomfortably. Kevin looked at me and seemed to think what I was thinking. How ironic that statement was! I have always felt that I didn't have a choice in this family.

The reason Kevin probably didn't offer to drive me home is that he recognizes my strength and healthy functioning as I do his. He didn't need to rescue me, and I didn't need to rescue myself. Kevin and I kind of got labled "the troubled children", and so Kathy, as the oldest, developed the facade of being healthy-functioning and perfect. My hearing loss (resulting from being born three months too soon) along with being the youngest enabled me to watch and observe a lot. Thus, I have gained much wisdom about people and relationships.

Perfectionism is the hardest thing I'll have to grapple with in recovery. In my quest to be perfect, I expected others to be perfect too. And since I'm more "on the ball" than most, I get disappointed easily.

In actuality, opposites are not that far apart. Children of privilege who are raised without much attention to their emotional needs, whose family always appears to be giving from the outside, are affected the same way as the kids whom are not given anything and are criticized and verbally abused. Balance is about finding the curve in the middle. If that were the one thing to remember, that would be it. Balance, balance, balance!

These limitations don't define who I am. It doesn't affect my self-esteem. Mom and Dad may not like some of the choices I make due to their limitations but they want the same thing. They want me to be happy and have the things that I want in life.

9/7/95

A lot of emotion came up while talking to my friend and alias therapist, Fr. John. Somehow I voiced being unhappy and I've never really come out and said it. We've both seen symptoms of it in my struggle with eating, home issues, family issues, etc. But somehow admitting to unhappiness seems unacceptable. It will come out as, "I'm OK", or "hanging in there". Society doesn't seem accepting of unhappiness.

I feel like a piece of my soul is shattered and I don't know how to fix it. It has come from my childhood but I don't know how one experience could affect me so much. My soul is shattered from having been sexually abused. I don't remember much but something was taken from me and I can never get it back.

It feels more painful to know that I continue the violation that's been done by self-inflicted abuse. By continuing to beat myself up, starve, and isolate, my soul becomes even more shattered.

9/27/95
Life is not lost by dying; life is lost minute by minute, day by dragging day, in all the thousand small, uncaring ways
Steven Vincent Benet

All we are is the result of what we have thought.
Anton Chekov

Reflection on Quality of life as a direct link to the sexual abuse:
10/11/95
It's like missing one of your senses. If you've never been able to smell, you don't know what that experience is like. I feel like I've been missing a significant part of my life, and if I don't confront this person, I'll never have it back.

No one but me knows the pain I carry and how it affects my life on a daily basis. I'd rather die confronting him than dying because he got the best of me.

10/14/95
I feel worlds apart from everyone in terms of having fun. I don't feel comfortable hanging out with friends in a bar or feeling like I'm being checked out. I can't relate to anyone of the opposite sex. It's not just about meeting people. That's difficult enough. When romance is in the picture, I freeze. I feel sick.

Khristian: A friend's commentary:
My maturity level is way beyond my years; that I'm probably the most healthy and stable person in my family. I know what I want and well aware of what I need and how to get it. Even

with all the bad things, this has made me a stronger person.

On control:
10/20/95
    I realized what my controlling nature is. I get stone silent and have a "don't mess with me" look that pushes people away from me. I also get sarcastic.

Day of Confrontation:
10/26/95
    My friends and confidantes, Marilyn and Fr. John, accompanied me. Marilyn had a good description for it. It almost feels like a baptism; a cleansing experience. We're going to the beach afterwards to commemorate.
    The Aftermath: I was unable to confront Bruce in person. He had conveniently moved to Florida two months before. I did not give up. I followed up with a certified letter.

10/29/95
    I have not received positive support from family, namely, Kathy and Mom. They do not understand. They think I'm selfish for not informing them. I did not tell them because I couldn't be dissuaded. I am especially disappointed in Kathy's reaction. This was about my own experience. Just because I'm a compassionate, open person who yearns to speak the truth and break all barriers does not mean I'm "engulfed" as she described it.
    Bruce is the criminal, not me, but they're condemning me. He should not get away with his crimes, yet they're helping by keeping it a secret. If they don't talk about it, then it never happened.

11/3/95
    The truth is they would have tried to talk me out of it. They at least succeeded in making me feel awful. I couldn't carry their weight and Bruce's too. The only reason they're mad is because I keep bringing up the issues for them that they want buried. They don't want me talking "outside" the family because, god, what would the neighbors think? They still have guilt and shame

issues. Sure, the family knows, but talking and healing are two completely separate issues. No one has healed. To not talk about it, is to pretend that it never happened.

Why should I talk to them anyway? They have never given me any indication that they would support me or offer me care and encouragement. I've always been brandished for my actions. And Mom's point about going to family meetings at the hospital to support me is fruitless because they (Mom and Allen) always went like it was a chore. It was with the air of, "when is this going be over with?"

They think this engulfs me but I'm not dwelling, I'm dealing. For me to keep addressing this issue means they have to look at their own stuff, and they would rather not.

11/4/95

I called my friend and former pastor, Fr. Bob. He caught me three times getting sucked into my family's lack of support. It doesn't matter what they think. What matters is my health. I did this for myself. It doesn't matter how I did it or whether they approve. This was my experience and about my relationship with Bruce. If I'm depending on their understanding, I'll have a lot of trouble staying well. I was engulfed but it was a real problem, and this is what I had to do to move on.

On receiving the confirmed receipt to my confrontation letter:
11/7/95

My heart was pounding and I was shivering. I felt like I wanted to throw up; my stomach was bubbling over. How interesting that it's something good rather than bad. I'm so excited. I've been smiling all night. It is so *liberating*. I feel I am truly free.

11/16/95

I'm thinking about throwing my scale out. It degrades my self-esteem each day I step on it. Why give it the power to determine how I feel? Why do I empower a hunk of metal to make me feel bad? It keeps me holding my breath. It has that nervous, "what next?" feeling to it. I can't really live freely when I'm a slave to the scale.

It makes me paranoid when people talk about outer appearances. I think it's very invasive. I know I've gained weight for my better health, but that doesn't mean my body is open for comment and scrutiny. Commenting on my body is making a comment about me. My body is an extension of who I am.

It was much easier for everyone when I was sick. When I change, I force other people to change as well, in how they relate to me. It's uncomfortable for them. It was never "our" problem. I've had to carry the burden of everyone else. That's where I feel weighed down. That's when I feel "too heavy". It's easy to become too thin, to become a disappearing act. But I stand up, and I speak up, and I continue to honor my convictions and myself. It takes guts and courage to stay well and to keep living.

It's all so easy; so easy to skip meals, to purge, to lose weight. It would be so easy to do that, but I'm not doing it.

11/22/95

I've been reflecting on Mom and who she is that makes her act the way she does. She doesn't seem to be a very happy woman. She doesn't appear to know how to relax or have fun. It's as if she's afraid to. Moreover, she doesn't seem to know how to think for herself. She always has to check with Allen before making a decision.

It takes more energy to be angry and to frown than it does to smile. She doesn't smile that often. Therefore, when she says she "works so hard", I can counter that with, "yes, you do".

I wonder how I became such a black-and-white person. Everything is extreme with Mom. Either I'm hanging out or I'm going off somewhere. I don't win with her.

I'm just glad I'm living and enjoying it. Mom doesn't seem to know how. She only knows how to do detail-oriented things like balancing checkbooks, paying bills, and straightening out the house. Whenever I invite her to do something with me, it's always; "I'm too tired".

I've been opening up more, but it seems like she's afraid to open up to me, so she doesn't respond. Or she'll act in a way that discourages me from opening up, but she's not aware of it.

I'm going way beyond her function level. She doesn't know how to relate to the adult Michelle. That was apparent in a stupid comment about soda today. She asked me not to open another bottle of soda since there were two already open. However, I don't like gingerale or Cherry 7-UP. When I told her this, she said, "too bad, drink the Cherry 7-UP until it's gone." That's ridiculous! I'm not going to drink something I don't like. That's talking to me like a child.

On the relapse of an alcoholic family member:
11/23/95

I'm learning from this because it helps me to see the other side of it. It helps me to see how it is for the family to deal with a sick family member. It's a similar situation. Did I do the same thing? My illness wasn't just controlling me; it was controlling the whole family. It actually feels kind of weird to not be the sick one. It's kind of a relief not to be in that spotlight anymore.

Thanksgiving Evening:

Tonight it was fun to look at old baby pictures. Me, Kathy, Mom, Kevin and Chrissy were sifting through them to pick and choose ones for ourselves. It was interesting reading notes on my speech therapy. My perfectionism was already evident by the time I entered kindergarten.

11/24/95

We spent more time looking at pictures and talking about family history up to the present day. I thought it was a little bold of me to ask how Dad had been as a father. It was forging into risky territory, but Mom was quite frank and open. She said he wasn't home much but it also had to do with the time. It's more acceptable for men to be home now. She also said he was immature but she didn't say it bitterly, just a matter of fact. They were both young. That was also attributed to the time. Nowadays, age 22 is pretty young to be married and have a family.

Tonight we're having cake and ice cream for Chrissy's birthday. This is really cool having quality family time together.

11/26/95

So much for quality family time. Kevin and I had a huge

explosion. It totally knocked me off my footing. It felt like everything was in slow motion like it wasn't real. I had this horrible sick feeling, like, "this can't be happening!" The words coming out of his mouth were unreal.

I talked with Fr. John yesterday after it happened and met with him today. He was so open, nurturing, so exactly opposite, that I felt my heart breaking. I see what I deserve to be treated like and it makes me so sad that I'm not getting it close to home.

I wrote a letter to Kevin, of which I'll send tomorrow. Fr. John affirmed its power for me. I'm not self-centered or self-absorbed. I'm taking care of myself by asserting my feelings.

We addressed why it is so hard to confront family members more than others. Why couldn't I stand up to Kevin? Because he's my brother and I love him. I don't want to lose a relationship with him. But I can't have a relationship with him if I can't be open with my feelings.

Saying not to cry, not to pout, not to be angry, is saying not to feel. Feeling equals living. The fact is, Kevin's the one who's being childish if he believes that not showing emotion is being strong.

If I'm at all childish, I think I have every right to be. It only took me years to catch up to everyone else. I'm *still* growing, learning, and evolving. It's as if they're asking me to be perfect. Gosh, I expected myself to be perfect! They're demanding too much of me.

What hurt me most was when Kevin made fun of the California memorabilia and FRIENDS display on my wall. Instead of getting to see the real me, he jumps to his own conclusion and considers it another childish thing. That wall represents my **dream**. It reminds me of where I've been and where I'm going. Everyone loves FRIENDS, but how many people have actually met them on a professional level? If I want to hang pictures of them, well, bless my soul!

What boggles my mind is that everything Kevin has ever said to me is no value to me now. Why should I believe him? Just last week he praises me on my progress, and this week he tears into me for being self-centered. He says one thing and then another. It doesn't mean anything. I never know what anyone is *really* thinking. I don't feel safe at all.

It just confuses me because how could all of them be wrong? But, like my friend Marilyn pointed out to me, I'm an artiste; I'm a different breed from them. They all sound alike because they're all the same. They think alike. I aspire to be an actress. That is definitely different. It's certainly not the safe choice. I don't follow their path so they don't understand me. They never will.

This is what it comes down to; what will make me happy in the long run? Where will I flourish the most? It's not here. I feel like I have a life waiting for me in California. I have to go out there and just experience life. Once I'm there, I can create my own family.

A reflection on Growing Up and Out:
11/27/95

My friend Cathy O. (a.k.a., Jackie O.) helped me to see that when I was a teenager, and everyone else was growing, I was stuck where I was. Therefore, I'm doing a lot of my growing now. Moreover, when I started getting better, no one else was. Now I'm healthier than everyone else is and they don't understand it.

A dream in the making:
12/3/95

When I was turning on the highway heading home after Opening Night, I saw a shooting star! It was right in front of me; I couldn't miss it. I made a quick wish, Hollywood, here I come! It just seemed ironic that I would see a shooting star on my "starring" night that it seemed to be a special signal to me from God, affirming my love for the stage.

On transition:
12/6/95

I have the power to choose what I want to keep and what to let go.

"Getting to Know You": Father and Daughter:
12/29/95

I had breakfast with Dad this morning. I told him I was

frustrated because I wanted him to understand, but maybe it only mattered that I understood. However, he said it's important for people to understand what you're going through.

It was interesting to me that Dad admitted he had just figured out his own expectations were what mattered compared to that of others.

Dad had breakfast with me because he wanted to, not because I asked him to. He even made the comment, "we don't get to talk alone too often."

A weird phenomenon is taking place. It's as if the whole family is realizing how precious our time is together.

New Year's Day
1/1/96

At mass today, the homily had been about how we can deliver ourselves from the attitudes and persons who threaten our peace and presence in God. Sometimes we have to shift our way of thinking to allow room for God's presence.

When I met with Fr. John personally, he related my going to California as me being delivered, me leaving behind old patterns and people who threatened my well being.

When bad things happen to good people:
Coming home from work, I fell asleep at the wheel and crashed into a tree on the corner of my street. It was 2:21 am.

I feel like God is with me telling me it will be OK. It's a time when I have to let go and let him take care of what's to be. It's not in my hands. He wants me to learn something from this. It may simply be to ask for help because then you realize how good people really are. I have to let people in.

1/6/96

Dad called me just a few minutes ago to check on me. Then he said that maybe this was a sign I should get a "day job" and that I should put my degree to use. No comment! I know what they see, but I don't plan to commit here. He mentioned the virtue of saving money but little does he know what I'm saving for. When I go to California, I can concentrate on getting a "real" job, but I won't have everyone breathing down my back.

On Inertia:

"We endure unsatisfactory situations because some of our needs are met there. If we take the risk, we might find that the rewards of a new beginning exceed any of our expectations."

Source Unknown

On fulfilling a Dream:
1/12/96

I'm frustrated because I want this to be a joyful experience. The sadness and fear is starting to overwhelm any excitement and joy I might feel. Aren't I supposed to be excited? Aren't I supposed to be jumping for joy? I'm going to California! I'm pursuing my dream! What is wrong with me?

I thought to myself how a scene in "When a Man Loves a Woman" relates to how I'm feeling. In it, Meg Ryan is telling Andy Garcia about her bad day. Nothing is particularly wrong. It just feels like a freight train has run you over. Nothing triggers it. It just comes and goes.

That's how I feel. I just feel awful without any explanation.

1/13/96

I'm still learning about food and my relationship with it. I want to think more about how I'm treating my body. I don't think I'm secure in my ability to be well. I think there's more awaiting me in California that I don't even know about. There *is* something out there for me.

Moving onward is bittersweet. It's exciting but it's scary. It's about starting all over again and leaving things behind. I'm not going on a vacation. It's OK to make mistakes. So often we're waiting for the perfect moment that we lose sight of what we're pursuing. If you're always waiting then the goal is elusive.

I never thought of my journey this way, but I've been given the opportunity of a lifetime. How many chances do we have to completely start over? I'm turning a new leaf on a whole new life; new people, new experiences, new trial and error. It's like being inside of a womb. You don't know what the world looks like until you enter it.

On Conflict and Confrontation:
1/14/96
    Intimidation does not equal strength and power. It is a sign of cowardice. I think I was stronger for holding my own with my boss. It's important to remember that.

1/16/96
    Controlling my weight is like controlling everything else. It's resistance to change.

1/25/96
    LA is going to be kind of special because I'll be getting to know the city in my own way. I had worried about the magical aura wearing off after being there for a while. On the contrary, it will just get more magical as I find favorite hangouts to call my own. It is so exciting to think about going there, but also recognizing, once I'm there, that's it. However, I had to arrive at this point.

1/31/96
    Everyone is saying how great I look and not necessarily because I weigh more. They say I look happy and peaceful; I have life in my face that's genuine. I don't look as pale or plastic. That's such a good feeling.
    I had concerns about California and how I would maintain my health. I'm going for my dream and myself. To me, that's a state of living. Having an eating disorder contradicts that. I'm sure I'll still have some "off" days, but that's all they'll be, temporary setbacks. There is no going back. California may be the last step in my recovery.

On being passionate:
2/1/96
    I learned from watching, "Mr. Holland's Opus" that sometimes we miss the most important message when we're focused on the "big picture". This man underestimated his influence on people because he never became rich and famous for his music.
    Maybe I'll never be rich and famous for my acting, but I'll

love teaching it. Who knows? The key is to have the passion.

On dealing with weight gain:
2/7/96
      I can't deal anymore. Although I exude peacefulness on the outside, I don't feel it inside. I don't get it. What do I have to do to make it complete?

      What I *don't* want is this body. I can't accept it. I won't. It's either take off the weight or face getting heavier. That's what's going to happen if I don't gain control. That's what happened before and I was miserable.

2/8/96
It's the small, every day things that are irritating me because I'm worried about larger, overwhelming issues.

2/9/96
      I'm going to keep going (with weight) until I feel better. I might feel better at 108 lb., but maybe not until 105 lb., or maybe 100lb. I know I'm pushing denial here, but I know that anything is better than where I am now (113lb). I hate the way I look. At least before, I knew I was skinny.

2/10/96
      I've made the connection between being gentle to myself and demonstrating assertive behavior versus aggressive behavior. It's significant to my wellbeing. I seem to possess more awareness and understanding than that of my counterparts.

      It's hard to accept the "forever" of recovery because often we project how we feel now onto the future. It might not always feel this bad. As I gain more awareness, and develop constructive ways of keeping self-destructive behavior to a minimum, the power of this disease will lessen. The good days will outnumber the bad. Additionally, there's always that one piece to remind you how painful it was. The anorexia will always be there but rather than *it* being the control, I can gain control over it. It's a part of me. I can't deny that.

      In homily today, the message was, "being true to yourself". Fr. John changed the refrain, "Are you doing the best you can?"

which is reminiscent of a report card, to "Are you being the best that you can be?" How you treat yourself reflects how you treat other people. In addition to trying to be the best we can be, we're also suppose to support others in being the best that they can be.

As long as I'm being true to myself, and you're conscience will tell you so, then you're welcomed in God's House. Everyone is welcome.

I was really upset by a comment made to me at work. This person said, "Michelle, you're gaining weight in your face, huh?" to which I replied, "gee, thanks." She responds, "no, that's good, isn't it? You were so thin before." The latter comment meant nothing to me. I immediately went to a mirror to check my face. All I can say is, not for long.

2/12/96
I went in the bathroom when no one was around and cried. It seems senseless to let someone's comment like that get to me; someone who really has no lasting importance to me. But it channeled into my insecurity and vulnerability about my body. I feel so incredibly fat. I hate the way I look right now.

2/14/96
I feel a little disappointed that I'm doing this (not eating). I don't even know why exactly- because of some stupid comment? I don't know what I should be appreciating. A part of me feels like I should be doing more, but I guess rather than appreciate what I have left, I want to numb my feelings by starving. It would seem easier to let go when everything is hazy.

2/15/96
Working hard at starving myself, and it doesn't seem worth it. I met with my friend Rachel for dinner. I feel sad that she feels she has no dreams or goals. She seemed to think it was *her* fault, but I assured her that it was just a plateau.

I feel like I should be absorbing more, doing more, but what? I am getting together more with people who matter most to me. It seems it's just waiting now.

Insight: comments about my weight throw me into an emotional tailspin because the scrutiny feels like sexual abuse, an unwelcome invader of my personal space, my body.

2/16/96
Last night Allen came home drunk out of his mind. Mom was already in bed. He kept asking where she was. He was banging around from room to room. Finally there was a large crash. Mom heard it but didn't get up. I got up to see. Allen had fallen out of his bed (in the guestroom) and the pillows were covering his face! I couldn't leave him like that for Mom to see, so I helped him get up on to the bed. I hope to god he was driven home. The car was missing. There is going to be mighty hell in the morning. Mom must have known he was drunk. How could she not?

It seems I came out looking more responsible for once. I'm healthy, strong, and responsible. Mom isn't accepting her role in choice making and Allen isn't accepting his irresponsible behavior concerning drinking. Both of them appeared embarrassed and ashamed about my intervening role last night. Perhaps I was enabling Allen by helping him, but I also felt like I couldn't leave him there.

However, the incident did help me see something in myself. I'm going to eat because I don't want to be found collapsed on a bathroom floor somewhere. Suddenly you realize how your self-destruction can affect other people.

Delusions of an Anorexic

Faulty Beliefs
I'll never starve/throw up again.

I'm weak

I'll never conquer this

If I show you who I am you won't like me

This recovery is too slow/too painful

Behaviors
Eliminating food groups
Excessive consumption of diet soda

Excessive gum chewing

Avoiding sit down meals

Feeling self-conscious about eating

Vomiting

Excessive exercise

Thoughts
I'd rather eat to little than to much.

Salads are healthy I don't have a problem

I'd rather be skinny and miserable than fat and miserable

I don't care

Characteristics
Black and White thinking

Minimizing positive achievements/Jumping to conclusions

Emotional responses "Should and Must"

Mislabeling and self-judgement/Expecting the worst

Self-blame and personalization

Making mountains out of mole hills

2/19/96
    Another unkind comment was made to me while I was at work. This person observed me eating some animal crackers and said she didn't know how I could eat and be so "bony". Which is it, bony or chunky? I chose to ignore her. My colleagues tell me I shouldn't feel bad for having done the right things: going to school, not having a kid, and going off to California.

2/20/96
    A part of me feels at peace. The idea of eating exactly what I want seems really appealing. I'm not always going to feel at peace with my body. That's why it's important to get help and receive support. I'm really tired of my body.
    What I'm thankful for is that I'm healthy enough that I no longer worry about whether I'll die in my sleep. I don't worry about passing out. I do wish I was thinner, but the cost is so great. You have to remember how it felt to be so weak, tired, and depressed. Life meant nothing more than what I was going to eat and how much I would weigh in the morning. The value of my life is not a number on the scale.

On sharing my story for the Lenten Homily:
2/21/96
    I am so thankful for being able to share of myself. I was surprised by the response of people. A lot of them approached me to say thank you and wished me luck. It felt really good to know I had an impact.
    I'm feeling really good about myself. These are the moments that make me want to get better and stay there. I feel like today was a triumph. I'm coming from darkness into light. I feel OK. I'm going to be OK. God will take care of me.

2/22/96
    I'm concentrating very hard on my hunger cues. I trust that if I listen to my body's nutritional needs then I won't have to worry about my weight. It will stabilize.

2/23/96
    When I was talking to Fr. John today, he asked me what I like to do. I couldn't think of anything right away, except dancing. It's been so long since I've done anything enjoyable. The last time I danced was at Kevin's wedding, and that was the beginning of my relapse.

On family being out of the loop:
    Even when I couldn't speak, my body screamed at them to get a clue. They just don't get it.

The mother/daughter struggle:
2/29/96
    It might not be until after I move that Mom and I will be able to have a relationship. Sometimes people resist change even if it's a healthy one. Mom might not like the changes in me. As long as I'm living here, I'm still a child. It doesn't matter that I'm 25 years old. I'm not what they want me to be. I'm way beyond that so we have these confrontations.

3/3/96
    Dad called to ask for my lunch order for when I get there later this afternoon. Now that I think of it, how different that is from Mom. She labels food, "don't touch", and Dad always makes sure that I have food I want to eat.

3/4/96
    I don't want to starve myself based upon someone else's ignorance. I feel better after writing. It helps me to remember why I want to stay well. Today I like what I see in the mirror. I shouldn't let anyone take that away from me.

3/5/96
    In a few weeks, I'll be grocery shopping for myself. While eating dinner I felt like, "this isn't me. I'm not supposed to eat. I'm anorexic." Every once in a while it seems foreign to me. And I'm not skinny anymore. I like my body; I guess being skinny is more of a habit than a desire. I'm trying to develop a new attitude towards food. Whenever I start to feel anxious, and either want to

throw up or not eat at all, I think of how good food is; how it's rich with vitamins and minerals to nourish and energize my body. Before, I only thought of how fat I'd become.

3/6/96
I'm treating food like medicine. I take it every 3-4 hours to prevent "side effects". Uncle Johnny is teasing me about LA. He joked, "no salt, only salad and alfalfa sprouts". I said, "I don't do that anymore. I eat".

3/8/96
Maybe after I'm gone, maybe Mom will realize I'm not the problem; all the things she blames me for.

3/10/96
I'm taking charge of my life by seeking opportunity in a more optimistic environment.

3/16/96
One of the steps of recovery is to give. You can't keep what you don't give away.

3/21/96
Fr. John gave me a little gold magnet of a cherubic angel. Its hands are on its cheeks and it's looking downward. I can put it on my refrigerator. He said he hadn't even made the food connection. It's kind of good to laugh about now, to have a sense of humor. I tried to tell him what he meant to me. He said the biggest sign was just seeing how I was taking care of myself. I had built my wings to fly.

Following my dream to California:
Go west, paradise is there, you'll have all that you can eat of milk and honey over there. You'll be the brightest light the world has ever seen, the dizzy height of a jet-set life you could never dream. Your pale blue eyes, strawberry hair, lips so sweet, skin so fair. Your future bright beyond compare; it's rags to riches over there (lyrics from "San Andreas Fault", Natalie Merchant's Tiger Lily CD).

Michelle Bahret

3/23/96

I am beginning a new life here in California and I turned 25 years old yesterday. It's a turning of a leaf and a new era. Getting ready to leave was hard. When Kathy called me, I lost my composure. I thought, if I can just get through this first step, then I'll be fine. I *need* to go through with this for my peace of mind.

Mom took me to the airport. When it was time to say good-bye, I felt so sad. Mom looked so lost and her face had such pain. It was heart breaking. We both cried and hugged each other. I watched her leave by herself, and wondered, what was the ride back going to be like for her?

My friend Khristian accompanied me on this trip for the first week, a nice vacation for her, and support for me. Last night we went to The Eclipse for my birthday dinner. It was amusing to people-watch. A bunch of rich and powerful people being fake and carrying on like they're in a show. Latti-da! Both Khristian and I noticed that there wasn't one unattractive person in sight.

Khristian asked for my opinion on a girl that was present in the restaurant. It was clear that she had anorexia. We talked about it. Khristian told me to be careful; that I can call her when I get discouraged.

3/24/96

Now that I live here, I'm not a tourist. I'm incredibly happy to be here. My freedom equals health and well being.

3/26/96

Just returned from Morton's where the post-Oscar party was held. We attempted to go downtown to try and get a glimpse, but everything was blocked off. I could see a little of the gold statues.

Khristian and I got a pizza and brought it back to the room to watch the Oscars. How neat it was, knowing that it was just fifteen minutes away.

Best Supporting Actress Mira Sorvino said exactly how I felt. As a child she was moved by performances she saw and wanted to touch people in the same way. And at the end,

Whoopie Goldberg said any kid wishing to be in the movies can be. You have the power.

It's so exciting to be a spectator. Yet, at the same time, I yearn to be on the other side.

From Country girl to City chic:
3/27/96
Starting to feel a little intimidated and overwhelmed. I just find that outside noise is so distracting. I get frazzled. To keep my nerves calm, I think it's a good idea to meditate.

3/29/96
It's the fist time I feel really alone. I feel like, once Khristian leaves, I'm free to starve myself. I'm already isolating.

3/30/96
Had a blast at Universal Studios today. However, despite the laughs, deep down I feel an ache of sadness and loneliness. Khristian leaves tomorrow and my immediate future is still unknown. I'm anxious about how I will make it through.

Over lunch, which I only took two bites of, I shared my anxieties with Khristian. She became alarmed and suggested maybe I should go home and wait six more months. I haven't even gone on auditions yet, and I'm already worrying about anorexia. Her thoughts were that there wasn't any way that I could handle both at the same time. I've set myself up for failure by walking right into it.

I can't go home. Even if I waited six months, I would still have to deal with being new to this city and the auditioning circuit. What would I do at home? And as far as therapy goes, there isn't anything that I haven't heard before.

So badly, I want to find a place in this town. It's not about a physical space but an emotional place. I try to think that every actor who is successful now has been in my place.

Remember God and keep him in your heart. He's still with you no matter where you are.

4/1/96
I should do what I came here to do, to act. If I'm not going

to do it, then I should go home.

It's like being a freshman all over again. I don't know where all the classes are, what books to buy, who the teachers are. I don't know anyone. It won't feel better until I start meeting people and getting involved.

4/5/96

The only thing that makes me happy right now is the weather. It's gorgeous. The weather back home is cold and slushy.

Keep praying. God will comfort you and keep you in his care. I couldn't have come this far to have something bad happen.

4/7/96

I have to find the courage to seek that message in other places. I have to open my heart to new people and experiences. There's a whole new world for me here if only I embrace it. The whole point is moving onward and taking risks.

The bravest thing is recognizing the time when you don't need help anymore. It would be so easy to keep going the same way. But it's like having blinders on. You can only take in so much. You have to widen your grasp. See more. Hear more. Embrace more.

It's scary to let in new people. I'm afraid of losing the old ones. As important as it is to move forward, the past still makes for who I am. It's a fine line. How much do you hold on to and how much do you let go? I guess time will decide that.

From baby daughter to adult:
4/10/96

I'm not going to base my choices upon what she thinks. Nor can I allow her to affect how I feel. I know this is hard for her too. I have to be patient. I pray to keep positive and keep my heart open.

Reflection of Young Hollywood:
4/11/96

It's cool because everyone is out for the same thing.

Although there's stiff competition, oddly enough, there seems to be a lot of support and team spirit.

Belly flop:
It's so hard. I feel homesick once again. I'm sitting here and I don't know what to do. I keep thinking, "when will I enjoy this? When will I stop feeling this way?" But I think I felt that way at the beginning of college too; only now I don't have home to run to every weekend. This is infinite. It's timeless. I don't know what will happen.

I can't let depression seize me. What would I be doing at home? I'd continue to have battles with Mom and Allen. I'd be dreaming of California and what could have been.

4/12/96
Looking at the HOLLYWOOD sign was stupefying. For years I dreamed of seeing it, and here I finally am! It seems so unreal.

4/13/96
If anything helps, it is the sunlight. I'm like a wilting plant that springs up once it feels the warmth of light.

4/14/96
Mom is shipping me my towels and sheets. She seems hesitant with sending all this stuff. I think she still hopes that I'll be coming back home after six months.

On leaving the Past behind:
People are always there to encourage you, but they also have their own lives to lead.

4/19/96
People are so ready to take you in out here. Look at Jane and Kirk, two wonderful people, and actors, whom I met through a connection. I'm basically a stranger to them but they've been good friends to me. It's like, "any friend of x is a friend of mine" type of deal.

Michelle Bahret

4/21/96
　　Mom found a book of mine in my room called, "when children are broken", and said she was very hurt by it. It almost seemed like I had planted it for her to find. I told her it wasn't about *her* and that I didn't leave anything for her to find.
　　It seems like, now that I'm here, a whole can of worms is opening up for Mom. Maybe finding that book was good. Now her healing can begin.
　　Mom seems very hurt and I hear a lot of helplessness in her voice. Our relationship is changing. She can't control me; she doesn't know where I'm at or what I'm doing any hour of the day. That has got to be very tough for her.
　　My new friend Frank commented to me that I was sent into his life for a reason. He has a feeling that he has to help me out in some way. I told him that I've been blessed with the people I've met. I never would have had a clue as to where to get the names I was given (industry sources). And, Louise's was just a random choice that night (Frank was my waiter one evening during my first week in town). His reply? "It always is."

4/22/96
　　I'm questioning what I should be doing for jobs. It's a scary feeling. The big question, "will I make it? Will I survive? Can I pull this off? Those are *three* questions, but they're a dark cloud over my head.
　　I can't feel guilty for what I've done so far. I've accomplished a lot and I'll continue to do so. I need some stimulation like a meal out, a movie, or a magazine. Those are small things in the big picture of life.
　　Don't whine about your situation, just *do*. Whatever you're feeling anxious about, find a way to absolve it. Feeling anxious about $? Get a job, any job. Don't worry about what Mom or anyone thinks. The large picture is that you want to be an actress. You have to eat until you get there. It doesn't matter as long as you have $ in your pocket.
　　Pray. Keep talking to God. He'll help you get through this. He'll help you find the answers. Trust and let go. Trust and yea will find.
　　I have to do my own thing. I moved to be able to do this.

The fact that you're here says a lot. Everyone knows why you're out here. They *expect* to hear that you're waiting tables. They know what the larger picture is. It will all pay off. Think of the people I've met already.

4/24/96
I received a very nice letter from Mom today. She told me that I have courage and high principles. She wants me to stick by them and not take the easy way out. Letters are great because people express things they wouldn't put into words. Mom validated me in that letter.

4/27/96
My first audition is today! No matter what happens, I'm just going to try and have fun, not take it too seriously. I'm thinking about what to do with the character. She's like me. New in town. A little naïve about the business. Innocent. She's younger than I am.

It feels good to know that things I've said to Mom are coming back to me. She told me about a workshop she attended at work that was about visualization and goals. Mom just thought I was being naïve, but she said much of the workshop reiterated things I had said! She even talked to the teacher about me!

4/28/96
Think in the present of all the things that you want to accomplish. Then ask yourself, what are the little voices that get in the way? Where and who did they come from? A little statement is enough to shoot down a dream.

5/3/96
I feel depressed now and I'm trying to figure out why. I bought food. I feel guilty. But I have to nourish myself! Not having food in the apartment makes me feel like I'm not worthy and don't deserve to eat. How is that going to affect everything else I do? You say you want to feel more at home, but keeping the refrigerator bare is certainly not going to feel homey.

As always, I feel like there's something I should be *doing*. But you need time to stop and smell the roses too. If you're always moving, doing, and rushing around, then how can you appreciate life and what you've done already?

I'm starting to become more comfortable with life in California. Every now and then, it still hits me; I'm in California!

> **Intro**: Kate McGregor Stewart: Actress and Acting Coach to Marisa Tomei, Jane, Kirk, Frank, and now me. She is a beloved mentor, a friend, and a "surrogate Mom".

5/6/96

I went to Kate's acting workshop. We did our monologues and I was so surprised by my own performance. I had commented to myself about how I'd love to do comedy. My monologue became very comical although it could have been very serious.

Everyone howled. I was surprised and pleased. What an exciting feeling! I was so nervous up until that point, not sure how I would play it. But once I said my first line, I was there.

Kate says I have great comedic style, and upon leaving, that I was so good and talented. I don't think Kate is the kind of person to be fake about that. So I'll believe her.

5/13/96

Los Angeles isn't a city to just hang out in. It's fun, but I came to LA for a purpose and I should always have focus of it.

On internal and external images of self:

It doesn't matter how anyone sees me but myself. The truth is, I'm never going to be a lion; I'll never have a roar, and I don't want to. I'm sick of people telling me to roar, to speak up. I've had to fight harder because of my quiet demeanor. I'm my own person now. Most of the time I've just learned to let things slide. I don't care about control. I am *not* meek, weak-mannered, or stupid. I will *not* ask for so-and-so's approval. I do *not* have to explain myself or who I am.

6/4/96

I saw Helen Hunt! It was over a week ago in a coffee shop. I was so excited. Moreover, the people I auditioned for were also there! Talk about seeing opposite ends of the spectrum.

Tonight I went out with people from work, including Kirk, Jane's friend. I feel more insecure. I couldn't offer any "colorful" coming of age experiences. I was just a do-gooder. It's like back in high school where I always seemed to be dismissed. It's hard to reveal who I am. I can tell what they're all thinking, "what is this Michelle all about?" but I'm not going to change who I am. I may not have had wild days, but I certainly had my demons. It's just not as easy to talk about as free drug use.

Interlude:

After my first week in town, and Khristian had gone, I stayed with Sonia, a former college acquaintance, who graduated a year behind me. I called her when I learned that she had just relocated to Long Beach in January, on a job offer that had materialized from an internship. We hadn't hung out in the same circle of friends, but we shared time together on school activities. We were both on the Program Committee, which planned educational, social and entertainment events for the college, we were both involved in Greek life, and in Peer Ministry, a student-run support group based on faith which had theme-oriented activities each week. Although we weren't close friends, we knew each other enough, but not so much that rooming together would be a threat to our relationship. I was not happy in my own apartment and Sonia was not happy in Long Beach. She wanted to be closer to LA that was more youth-oriented. However, both of us had a slight problem. Sonia's sister Kelly was coming out to California to go to school in the fall. Of course she'd want to stay with Sonia. It would be no problem if it were just the two of them, but who else would want to accept that? And my problem was that I wanted a roommate but I didn't want to just go with anyone. Knowing some familiarity was a comfort. So we struck a deal. We'd get an apartment together, and Kelly could stay for one semester and her dues would be paying the utilities. Sonia assured me that it was temporary and I reinstated that the situation would be reevaluated at the close of the semester.

At the time, it seemed like an innocent deal. It even seemed like it would be fun. But then I still held this fantasy reminiscent of "Melrose Place" (without the backstabbing), of living in an apartment building with all young people starting out. And the cherry on top was that we literally lived one block north of the famed Melrose Avenue strip.

Not until Kelly came into the picture did I realize how disastrous the arrangement could be and was. However, I didn't think I could change my mind or readjust the negotiation and nor did I think that I could move. Either way I felt caught between a rock and a hard place. We had a one-year lease and there were still nine months to go. I was not going to start a conflict now. To complicate matters, I liked Kelly, but my resentment grew when it became apparent that she was going to become a permanent fixture and Sonia wasn't making any adjustments herself. It didn't occur to me that Sonia should have been solely responsible for Kelly if Kelly couldn't support herself. There are such things as residence halls and student loans. Paying utilities in Southern California, where it's hot ten months out of the year, means dip shit. The bottom line was that Kelly and Sonia had used me and it was a major blow to my recovering ego.

6/20/96

Sonia and me went to the infamous Fermosa Café, the hot spot during the golden era of Hollywood. It is walking distance from the apartment. I had two Pearl Harbors. It was so much fun. We talked about everything and at a rapid pace. Maybe I should change my attitude about alcohol...

Sonia said she was quiet upon going into college but became a more social person through drinking. Alcohol breaks down barriers.

I was sick from drinking the Pearl Harbors. Back home, the room was spinning and the alcohol didn't agree with the food I had eaten. After trying to dance and stay standing up, Sonia suggested, "maybe it will be easier if you just made yourself throw up." A green light went on in my head. I had wanted to throw up but felt I couldn't with Sonia there. How liberating! After worrying about getting caught by whomever over the years, I threw up in the presence of another person. Sonia says she has done it "millions of times".

I wonder how many girls at school did this. I thought I was

the only one, and low and behold, whole sororities were doing it at keg parties! The new pledges were actually taught how to make themselves vomit. I can see how throwing up alcohol can easily make a crossover to throwing up food. It's a quick fix. Feeling sick? Feeling too full? No problem, just get rid of it.
A thought of clarity in the midst of obsession:

> Eating is about living. Living goes way beyond the size of your hips.

Struck by Cupid's Arrow: my first serious crush:
6/28/96
> Usually guys send anxiety through my body, but I actually dream of kissing him, of being close to him. It feels like it would be safe. I don't think it takes too much to fall in love with someone. I know enough to see that he's kind, gentle, warm, sensitive, funny, and easy-going. He's not threatening at all. He doesn't even seem to have sex on the brain like most men do (ok, maybe I'm pushing it here).

> How do I let Kirk know these things? That he makes me feel warm and safe inside? Does he see me as a girl or like a "sister"? I wish I could tell!

6/28/96
> I saw Kirk at Jane's house. She wasn't there. He was there by himself doing his laundry. Meanwhile, he was lying in the sun on the porch. I hadn't expected to see him. It was perfect.

> We talked for an hour while I waited for Jane to return. I had my proofs back and he picked out what he liked. It was a chance to probe for a little personal information. He asked if there were anyone back east. I said no. I added that it was a good thing too. There was nothing to hold me back. However, why couldn't I return the question? Is *he* seeing anyone? Does he *want* to?

7/10/96
> I saw Kirk tonight at work. I can't help but smile all the time. At one point I couldn't stop laughing. It was like I was drunk or something. Maybe that's what love feels like.

7/16/96
I feel myself sinking within. Even the way I talk. I don't feel as articulate. It's more difficult to express my ideas. I'm homesick because I ache for the people who know me inside and out. I'm finding it tough to loosen up with people. I guess it's the boundary factor.

8/4/96
Spoke to Cathy O. for the first time about Kirk. She advised me to lay low and let time take its course. He knows the interest is there. After being on OLTL (One Life to Live) he's probably used to girls' attention. I'm different. I'm not the dumb, ditzy girl who is only into her looks. I'm much deeper than that and I hope he can see that.

On paying a visit back east:
8/23/96
I feel this pressure to look a certain way; I'm from LA now, but no one expects me to look ritzy or lavish. Not that they would want you to.

8/28/96
You don't have to be aggressive to move ahead. All you need to have is dignity and class, which you've got. I carry myself with grace and poise. Audrey Hepburn was all class and grace. Look at what she achieved. Don't let anyone ever make you feel like a wimp just because you seem quiet and non-responsive. You have all the tools you need to succeed, Michelle.

8/31/96
It's been so exciting to be back, but then as the days go by, I realize I have to go again. I have to go back and face what's so hard; the reality of my life. It has been such a hardship dealing with all the elements of California and what it means to act.

I visited my good friend, Fr. John. I was able to be myself with him. It was such a relief not to paint an illusion. I told him what I was dealing with; smoking pot and drinking, and how that whole environment exists in my own apartment. I'm extremely uncomfortable with Sonia, and now Kelly's use of it. They can choose to use it, but I don't want to be around it. I may have tried smoking and drinking, but it only made me more aware that it's *not* me. People who say alcohol and drugs help them to loosen up and be more sociable are just making excuses. It takes a lot of strength *not* to give in. And, if you can be manipulated by drugs and alcohol, how does that speak for the rest of your life?

    I've only seen it twice, but I've hated seeing Sonia stoned. Moreover, I did not feel comfortable with her philosophy of it "opening your mind". Openness comes from a *conscious* state of mind; not when it's altered! Any revelations you have under the influence of pot are not reality-based. I understood why I hated seeing Sonia stoned; because it wasn't her. She wasn't real, but she was trying to justify it. Truthfully, you look like a fool when you're stoned.

    This may all sound judgmental but I'm not trying to be righteous. I don't know how to handle this because I know it will sound upright. However, how many times has Sonia come off being superior? She seems so proud of being blunt, but the way I see it, she doesn't have it figured out at all. What I detest is her superior presentation with the phoniness behind it. It's not real. It's not from the heart. The fact that I can remember her inspiring quote from graduation ("we don't take risks to escape life, but to prevent life from escaping us"), and she can't, should explain it. And, as Fr. John pointed out, which journal would people rather read? My journal that has described all the struggles, pains, and triumphs? Or Sonia's that presents the American Dream but is written from an altered state of mind? I speak from my heart. My writing is real. Sonia's isn't because maybe she doesn't have faith from what's in her heart. But, most people would rather hear Sonia's story than mine because it's easier to hear. It's easier to get pumped up. However, real people, real people with real struggles would embrace my story. These are the people who are not afraid to be themselves. Honestly, I would rather be alone in this world and be true to myself, than sacrifice my values and beliefs, just to have tons of friends. What friends would they be, anyway?

On parent strife:
9/1/96
    I have concluded that as long as they put the entire responsibility of communication on my shoulders then they don't have to see their own faults.
    I can't change who they are, but I can change how I react. It just reminds me of why I left. It was no mere coincidence that as soon as I left that environment, my health got better. I transformed my looks. They might see that too. They see I'm looking better than ever, I have more confidence, and I'm doing well on my own. That must be difficult, despite it being positive. It pretty much says,"I can get along without you". I can learn to live my own life and enjoy it and not allow people's *stuff* to drag me down. I have to be happy with myself first. You can always stand up for yourself by choosing to eat.

9/1/96
    Did I use this trip to run away? I'm refreshed. I'm not really eager to confront LA again, but I have a clearer sense of whom I am and what to expect of myself.
    I think I'll be a lot happier just concentrating on my own life and what I need to do to feel happy and fulfilled. Go to work, acting classes, and be around people who excite and stimulate you; not criticize or drag you down. Find a quiet place for yourself where you can listen to your inner voice. Sometimes you don't know what works for you until you try it.

9/3/96
    I have to give myself a chance and not give up. There's too much opportunity. I should go to church. I can find people there who are more like me, and not into partying. I need someone to talk to.
    My cousin Jena sympathized with me. She said there's enough stress besides tackling the dream. You endure a different environment, lifestyle, eating habits, etc., and there's no one familiar to talk to.

9/4/96
    I feel absolutely sick to be back here. I never thought I

would feel this way about LA. It hurts so much to know that just a matter of hours ago, I was home. But it's not really your home anymore. You're here now. Mostly, that's what pisses me off. I'm here by choice. I'm so angry that I hate it here. I have to stick it through. I do definitely need to talk to someone, so that these feelings do not eat me up.

I'm not worrying about anything. Give yourself a break. I'm so tired of worrying about what people will think or how they'll react to my actions. Start concentrating on you. Do what makes you feel happy. You're no good to anyone if you don't love who you are. You have to take care of you first.

9/9/96

How can I be so happy and sad at the same time? I'm happy because I'm so excited about meeting new people *and* being healthy. I'm still doing so wonderfully. No symptoms! Yet, I'm really sad for that same reason. I'm really moving onward. There is no looking back.

Just remember, I could never have come to California or had the strength to pursue my dream, if I were still living with anorexia.

Interlude: 3-month gap due to lost material.

New Year's Day
1/1/97

Parents are more apt to point out disapproval than approval, for reasons I cannot understand. I can't really know the degree for which Mom feels proud. She may never tell me. I may never hear it. But I can turn it around by affirming her or trying to be understanding.

1/3/97

I tackled my fear of airports by driving into LAX to pick up Khristian who is visiting for the week. It was packed and I had to drive around a couple of times until I saw her.

We went to Spago, famous for the post-Oscar party, for her birthday dinner. Although we were seated in Siberia, it was fun just to do it. Now I can anticipate being there after the Oscars.

1/5/97
    Food finally seems to be falling into its perspective category. Today we went to the boardwalk in Venice and then headed to Beverly Hills where we stopped for lunch. Again, I ate for nourishment and enjoyment.
    Khristian and I love the California lifestyle, read the same books, prefer the same clothes, and we jot things down in our journals. She jokes that she was born on the wrong coast. She wants to migrate this way.
    After reflecting for the umpteenth time, I said, "I hope I'm not boring you to death." She shrugged and replied, "You're in love." I never thought of myself being like that but it is true. I've never felt this way about anyone before. I don't fall for people very often. I've never felt such calm and peace as when I am in company with Kirk. And when I feel safe to be me, then only the best comes out. As the saying goes, "love makes the world go 'round."

    Love is patient. Love is kind. It does not act unbecomingly. It is not provoked. It does not take into account a wrong suffered. Love believes all things, hopes all things, endures all things. Love never fails.
                                        1Corinthians 13: 4-5, 7-8

On going against type:
1/6/97
    I might think about choices where I don't know how to feel. Since so much of my life has been about drama, I'd like to take a turn with comedy. Maybe my risks and against-type are not sexual or confrontational scenes. I know how I feel in those situations. But it's taken me a long time to remember how to laugh. I think my risk is allowing myself to show my funny side. That is surely a vulnerable place too.

1/8/97
    My scene partner had this to say about my withdrawal from the showcase: don't wait to be perfect to get up. You learn by doing. I do not feel ready now, but don't let that detract from exploring and rehearsing more material.

There's no such thing as a failure who keeps trying.
Unknown Source

To be or not to be? Unrequited love:
1/8/97

I want to have faith, and keep hoping, but at the same time, I want to let go and move on. Don't give away a good friendship based upon what you feel are lost expectations.

1/10/97

Katie affirmed my talent. Her word of the day was on impeccability; taking the extra step. Finish the job. Don't leave it for the next person. Do what your instinct tells you. Some examples: if you think the door is unlocked, get up and lock it. It only takes a minute. If you're the last person to use the toilet paper, replace the roll. If you're picking up litter, and you see another piece, finish the job.

Taking actions like these affirms our word. We keep our word by going the extra mile.

Never make assumptions.

On giving up my "day" job:
1/12/97

There's always a reason for the way things happen. Why don't I use this time to actually enjoy California? I haven't really done so up until now. I've always been concerned with living and what I need to do. I can use this time to enjoy my freedom.

Fear is instilled for a reason. Don't run away from it. It's there to teach you something. Acknowledge it and thank it for being there. However, don't let it overpower you. Learn the lesson and move on.

1/13/97

I think Kirk is a special person who showed me a different way. That's his gift to me. He's already served a purpose in my life, and that may be all there is.

Michelle Bahret

On dealing with my blocks of fear and doubt:
1/23/97
My problem is I'm keeping myself stuck in a circle. The world is revolving around me and I don't know how to jump in. Just take one thing and run with it.
1/24/97
Jane's feedback for me is that I have the ability of manifesting what I want when I need it, when I decide to do it. You have seen over and over again that once you decide to put yourself out there, things come to you. The Universe will help you once you open your self up. Things have a way of taking care of themselves, of course, with a little help from you.

Thinking backward to move forward:
1/26/97
I don't even know how I lost the weight, but I can understand now, how deceived I was by my eating habits. I had no concept of reality. I try to remember the obsessive thinking; the longing to eat something normal but being unable to. Now I can't even imagine it.

My thoughts on sexuality:
1/27/97
I don't feel bad about being a virgin. I'm glad I haven't given it away. It's something I still have and I can make a choice I don't have to regret. But I'm also aware that my choice is provoked somewhat from the abuse. I wonder if I hadn't been abused, would I feel differently about my sexuality? I'm a virgin out of respect for my body as a result of what happened. The only negativity I feel is that I feel partially stunted in my emotional growth. The part that feels damaged thinks there's something abnormal about this. However, if I decided never to have sex at all, there's nothing wrong with that. It's not the basis of life. OK, so it is literally, but the world is not going to go extinct if you don't participate in procreation. What I don't know, I can live without. But I do think the right person will come along. Maybe I'll be blessed with never having to endure bad sex because I will have waited to be with someone I really care about and vice versa.

Counting Bones

1/30/97
     Life is not a consistent happiness but a series of moments. You learn to have appreciation for them when you begin to cherish that there will be many more to come. Happiness IS the way. There is no way TO happiness.
     Michelle, you have courage and stamina. You have always been real. Some people are going to reject you because of it. They are threatened for some reason. As long as they have the last say, they can feel in control. They don't have to face their insecurities if they can keep accountability off of themselves.

2/2/97
     I feel scared and out of control. I called Marilyn who was encouraging. She says she doesn't worry about me. There is no time frame on fulfilling dreams. In the meantime, you do what you have to do.
     I went to church. The homily was about surrendering. Lose yourself. Hand your fate over to God. Let him help you. You usually don't know the why of something until you do surrender. Then the answers come.

2/7/97
     Michael was my partner tonight in an exercise. I was happy because I had wanted to know her better. First, we had to study each other's faces nonverbally. Then we each closed our eyes and relaxed. After that, we each took a turn watching each other while the other person's eyes were closed. Finally, we pictured painting that person's face and putting on that face. The results were amazing!
     While I felt more open, serene, and tall, Michael felt more caged and enclosed. She said she became more aware of everything, like she was observing. She had noticed that my eyes are feline-shaped. Thus she felt like a cat and the way a cat takes things in. How interesting! She became me and I became her! It just goes to show that you can reach those places. The lesson behind this is, go to the truth of the matter.

Michelle Bahret

On my increasing discomfort with my living environment:
2/10/97
    I need to say something because it affects how I feel and my way of being. When a problem arises, I feel even more insecure and taken advantage of. This is where I live, and I shouldn't feel uncomfortable in my own space. I feel like a stranger in many ways, and this isn't what I worked for.

    There has to be alternatives. It's not fair to be paying half the rent and only receiving one third of the share. It's about me not wanting to feel taken advantage of and used. I can't feel that in my own apartment. I've worked too hard to make a home for myself.

    We've all experienced bad judgements. Ask anyone. Anyone will try to take advantage if they see an opportunity. It's not personal and I shouldn't feel ashamed. I am a good person with a good heart. I haven't lost anything.

2/14/97
    State how it feels in your body first. Pause. State your fear. Each week we begin class with opening news in which everyone is welcome to share their news or just check in. It's a time for sharing audition experiences, announcements, feedback, and even networking. It is a usual occurrence for people to be looking for an apartment, a roommate, a car, etc. We all look out for each other. These are my peers and also my competitors but I find that we don't really compete against each other. I think it is a misconceived idea that actors are egotistical and superficial. Such people do exist, but I haven't encountered many. It is actually very rare to be going up for the same roles because everyone is so different.

    After the opening news session, Katie begins warming exercises with what are called sentence completions. Kate spontaneously throws out a phrase, which we each have to respond to from our inner gut reaction. First, we have to say how it feels in the body and then connect it to the phrase. Tonight, the phrase was "I fear…"

    This was my response: "I feel like my stomach just dropped to the floor like a falling elevator shaft. My mouth feels dry. My head feels like it's stuffed with cotton. My arms are tingling and my hands feel clammy...I fear being attacked." Do not punctuate the two clauses with "and"; it's a device to fill in the space and it also disconnects the thought from the physical sensation. When you make the connection, it leads you to a truthful place.

No one ever questions what you say because your inner response will always reflect your outer response. Whatever the sentence completion is about will bring up the emotion. Its purpose is to connect circumstance to feeling. Thus if I need to feel fear in a scene, I can use this sentence completion to help me get there.

After sentence completions, we dance to two or three songs that vary from 40s swing dancing to jazz to slow and seductive, to silly and playful. The latter is always fun because we all laugh and get out of breath. The dancing helps loosen up the body and is always good to do before an audition or to break out of a rut. Once the warm-up is completed, the class work begins followed by scenes and monologues people worked on outside of class. You're supposed to present work at least twice a month. After presenting a scene tonight, Katie once again confirmed I had a gift for comedy.

Continuing conflict on the home front:
2/15/97
I think I've been more than generous and fair. It seems once I put my foot down then I'm the one who has a problem. I'm not being silent or agreeable or the nice girl anymore.

I have to cultivate ways to make myself be heard loud and clear. In the meantime, I am NOT feeling guilty. Anyone who is guilty immediately wants to turn the tables and point the blame.

In response to Sonia's remark that if I felt a certain way, then it was my issue:
2/16/97
Sorry, but if I feel something, it's a reaction to something. In regard to what I've taken away from this:

I did learn something, and it wasn't that I should take more initiative or be stronger, but to stick by my convictions and personal truth.

Another sentence completion, "Congratulate me for...."
2/21/97
    First, congratulate me for standing up to my roommates. Second, congratulate me for maintaining a 30-pound weight gain in an industry where image costs everything. The class greeted me with silence. I looked up in time to see the compassion on Kate's face, but I couldn't gauge the rest of the class. It seemed interesting to me that no one applauded me in the same way one would for a person losing weight. Weight loss is so admirable but does anyone see how weight *gain* can be so incredibly hard? Either way, you're dealing with a fat person.

    Katie advised me not to silverbox; meaning not to shut down, after hopelessly flailing about in my scene tonight. Remain open to direction.

    I saw myself pushing people away again. Cheryl came up to me and said, "I loved your share." I immediately replied, "I almost skimped on that." I didn't really embrace what she had said. And when she playfully quipped that I was "foxy" in my velvet, I shot back, "*you're* the fox (she had leopard print on)."

    Another classmate, Kris, told me I was funny. My facial expressions are interesting to behold. I remarked that I was surprised because the scene hadn't been as funny as it was the week before. She replied, "you're funny." That made me feel so good because it demonstrated that my good qualities still come through even if the scene shouldn't.

2/27/97
    The sentence completion in class was, "a degrading moment for me was when..." I waited until the very last minute to respond. I couldn't escape what came up for me. My cheeks burning, my stomach sinking, and my legs weak, I told about the time I collapsed in the hallway of a very busy student union. I had lost control of my bowels for all of my class to see.

    By contrast, I was the first to respond on the next sentence completion. "I delight myself with...collecting seashells on the beach." The purpose of this exercise is to teach you how to pull up emotions when you need them. If you remember how a certain experience felt like, and what it felt like inside the body, then you can pull up any feeling. No one is acting in his or her sentence completion. Everyone is honest and true. It comes from a real place. No one questions or judges it.

3/5/97
    I have come to recognize what the whole apartment conflict was about for me. I see it as my own self-sabotage. I said yes, everything is fine when I really meant to say no. My instinct told me so.
    I'm still trying to get healthy and I make mistakes. There was a pay-off in this scenario. It kept me gritting my teeth. It kept me stuck. It affected my whole self-worth to the point that I couldn't speak up. Well, now I know to be aware and cautious of those tendencies.

On making the decision to return to the East Coast:
3/16/97
    I think a lot has to be said for facing family and personal demons. I thought the answer had been to separate myself from them. But maybe now the time has come in which I learn to see beyond the limitations.

My thought lies between my dream and me:
5/17/97
    Sometimes you don't see something until it comes back to you.

5/18/97
    Simple doesn't mean boring. It's a way of being. Being uncluttered allows more of you to come through.

5/25/97
    I relish comments, "you look great", as opposed to, "you look thin". It's weird. There was a time I would have cringed because I wasn't supposed to look good. I didn't want to look good. I wanted to be frail and thin. I didn't know how to receive good attention. But now, hearing those comments helps me to keep on going. I do look better!
    People are noticing different things. A few weeks ago,

Chris said she never noticed how long my eyelashes were. Yesterday, Karen tells me she never realized how blue my eyes were. It's because, not only was I malnourished, but my thinness was a big distraction. Now people can see beyond that. I'm not so skinny. They can see more of me that was so carefully tucked away.

    I know more of me too, so there's no place to really go. I think about losing weight but I haven't acted on it. I feel too good. Food itself is a good experience. I remember hating family gatherings. I would get so lost in the food. But that's because I didn't know how to spend time with them. I didn't know myself so I couldn't *be* myself. Yesterday, I enjoyed eating and being with the family. I even helped myself to a second serving of a dessert. That wasn't the case a few years ago.

Author's Note:
    This next entry was based upon a revelation I had about myself in relation to the opposite sex. Several months before this, I disclosed my personal struggle from an eating disorder and sexual abuse to Kirk. I considered it a milestone because it was the first time I had told this experience to a male, that I even had a male friend was exceptional indeed. I think my reasoning for the disclosure was to test the tepid waters and I was rewarded by a compassionate and gracious response. I wanted to validate that I was Ok with the opposite sex but in actuality I wasn't. It's important to note that Kirk was a completely platonic friend and was attached to someone else.

5/29/97
    There was a reason why I told Kirk about myself and he was absolutely right in his interpretation of that. I *thought* I was saying, "it's okay", but what I really said was, "no, this is not okay. I'm not ready". Kirk saw this even if I didn't. He was the best person I could have asked for. He was actually being a good friend by recognizing this and being respectful of it.

    If I jump into a relationship, with anyone, not just Kirk, it ultimately means s-e-x. Even marriage. This isn't a 50s sitcom world we're living in.

6/23/97
    Kirk recommended a book for me to read called, *Hope for the Flowers*. It's such a beautiful, lovely story; all about finding your place in the world and inner beauty. It's also a story of friendship and love. It speaks so much to me how Kirk perceives me. Literally, a caterpillar struggling to become a butterfly!

On strife and friction at home:
6/28/97
    You have to get back to California. Maybe training myself with this mental attitude will help me in Hollywood. This is about survival. I am not going to get kicked down. I have to tune it all out. Don't get sucked in, and if you do, don't beat yourself up.

Painful growing pains:
6/30/97
    The situation is really sad. We can't accept this time together to be mother and daughter for a while. I'm going back to California in a year, and then she'll be worrying and missing me again. Well, what about NOW? Why does living at home have to be so miserable?
    She's unhappy so she projects it on you. She can't even understand what you say because she's on a different plane. It's not worth stating these things because she won't understand. It's like a foreign language.

7/2/97
    I've been experiencing bodily distress over the past week. I'm feeling fat and battling the temptation to starve. I feel like I'm eating too much.

7/3/97
    Every now and then I feel like I'm on a set. When I was walking outside tonight, my surroundings seemed so surreal; like everything was a prop on a soundstage. The rustling breeze seemed strange too. Hundreds of fireflies pierced the darkness.

In the aftermath of a terrible fight with Kevin:
7/9/97

I recognize when abuse is coming. How do I know it? I always feel like I have to vomit. Ordinarily, I would be vomiting. I'd be vomiting all day. But I got through it. I felt like I was going to die in the awful aftermath, but now that I've written a little bit, I feel better. It won't control my day.

Just when I think it's safe and okay to be myself, something like this happens. The "truth" comes out. How they see me comes out.

7/9/97

Why is he getting to me? Maybe I still question the truth. I know the things he said were not true. He doesn't know what he's talking about. He doesn't know whom he's talking *to*.

7/10/97

Just about everything they say against you is an element of jealousy and wonder. You ARE great, but in a different way. Because you don't fit the mold, they think you're wasting your potential and talents. And because you ARE different from them, you suffer your own persecution. But, you'll keep on marching girl, in the face of adversity. They will try and keep you back, but you will keep charging forward. And when they look back, they'll see how dedicated and "right on" you were but they will never admit it. You will never tell them, "I told you so", because you'll remain generous and humble.

7/15/97

Family is incapable of understanding my mission so I need to surround myself with people who do. An alchemist is someone who keeps pounding granite until she hits gold.

7/20/97

Mom and me had a weekend alone together because Allen was away. It was really nice. There was no conflict at all which leads me to believe that perhaps Allen is the one who causes it. By herself, I don't think Mom really cares.

Counting Bones

7/23/97
    I spotted an anorexic in the mall today. She was a woman of about 28 years. She couldn't have been more than 80 pounds. No butt, no hips, and her arms were like matchsticks. She could have had cancer or AIDS but I guess anorexia. Why? Because she was a fashion plate. There are the anorexics who hide their bodies in baggy clothes and then there are the anorexics who flaunt their thinness in all the hippest clothes. I belonged to the latter category. I don't think cancer victims or AIDS-afflicted would flaunt their thinness from illness. It's a different feeling. You don't choose to be thin. It's something that happens to you. I don't think it' something that people with cancer or AIDS would enjoy or be proud of. They want to look healthy again. It's in reverse with anorexia. You love the thinness and control of it. Being healthy means being fat.
    The weird thing is that she sounded normal. She seemed like she was functioning all right. I guess this reminds me of what too thin is. You kind of get lost in it. You don't see it when you're in it.

7/26/97
    Why can't someone have a truly blessed life? Why can't someone be perfectly happy his or her whole lives? Why does pain and loss have to enter the picture? Can't we learn and be strong just from being happy? Can't happiness be built upon happiness?

On being embarrassed about my crush with Kirk:
7/27/97
    I thought I knew that Kirk was the person for me. Even if the time had been wrong, there would be a day. However, I was wrong, and now I feel embarrassed that I shared such certainty with my friends. It makes me not want to share again. But Michelle, that was your process! It was exciting to experience those feelings, the wonder, magic, and dreaminess of it. It was essentially your first love.

7/28/97
    I recognize how much calmer I'm becoming. My center is

becoming really quiet and tranquil. I'm focusing on other things. It's important to have a balanced life and not become obsessed with all the details. Learning to center yourself, to find your quietness within your soul, is going to be a tool you will need in Los Angeles. That is something you have struggled with but inner strength does not change with geography. Be mindful of the goals you do achieve. You will accomplish goals that weren't even goals to begin with.

8/2/97
When you're walking, and it's only you and God, the truth of your feelings become crystal clear. You have to weed out the doubts and fears to hear that soft murmur in your heart and to feel that slight flip-flop in your stomach. Then you have to be honest with yourself. That gut feeling is your truth, and when it's God speaking to you, how can it be wrong?

On making the decision to move out:
8/5/97
I need to be on my own to keep blossoming, growing, and branching out. I need my energy. On the same token, Mom needs her time too. For some reason, she can't do it when I'm here.

On the temptation to return to California skinny:
Katie wants to be assured that all her students are healthy and sound in mind. You can't give your full attention to class if you're not taking care of yourself. You can't have your career. But most importantly, you can't have your friends and loved ones. Katie loves you as a person first. She doesn't value you just as an actor. But each person- Jane, Kirk, Katie, etc. holds you responsible for the state of your health. Don't think for a minute that you need your illness to draw their attention to you. They already know how strong and smart you are. You don't need to relive the experience to show them. The eating disorder is not you. Why do you want it to re-enter your life? What do you want it to say for you? Why does it seem attractive to go back to California noticeably thinner? What do I derive from that?

More on the "Kirkster":
8/6/97
      I still wonder what's going through his mind. He never told me. In response to a letter I had written about how I felt towards him and what had actually occurred, he said he was flattered, intrigued, and curious. He told me he would write back but he never did. Guys don't write letters. I shouldn't be too disappointed with him. However, I do think that he wouldn't be intrigued or curious if he didn't feel some sort of connection himself. Those are such open-ended words. They are words that entice a person's interest, not deflect it.

      I used to think that maybe I was wrong in perception; that because it felt too comfortable to be around him, then it couldn't be real. I was just infatuated. But infatuation is fleeting; you've felt this way for a long time. Moreover, every time you try to turn away from it, something inside draws you back to it. It's precisely because you feel so comfortable, that it is the real thing. I'm trying too hard. I'm thinking too hard. I have to relax. Don't think, just do. And don't do what doesn't feel right.

8/7/97
      According to Mom, I'm a disgrace; a horrible, ungrateful person whom she's very ashamed of. If Nana were alive, she'd be ashamed too.

      Some families shouldn't be together. My friends are my family. The only thing I have in common with family is blood. I am completely foreign to them.

      I made a very big effort to reach out to Mom. It led to an escalation of further insults and accusations. I held her hand, looked her in the eye, and said, "if you can understand nothing else about me, then know that I love you." It led to quiet talking but the voices just started rising, rising, and when I put my hand up and said, "stop", she just continued. What else can I do? I know now, at the bottom of my heart, that I did my absolute best. My body woke up this morning weak and shaking but it's gone now. I'm replaced with an inner sense of peace and strength. I did what I just did to know that I could be well again. My body, mind, and spirit have been weakened dangerously. But I will begin to restore myself. I will not look back with any regrets. And it doesn't matter what she tells anyone about me because I know the truth.

Sometimes I wonder why this is happening. It's one thing after another. Something good happens followed by something bad. It makes me wonder if I'm not missing something.

In terms of eating, my pattern lately has been skipping breakfast, eating a small lunch, and skipping dinner. My weight is down to 113. I weighed 125 in California. How buxom and healthy I was. Ugh! I was chubby.

8/13/97

I'm getting full on less food. Some foods I can only eat a bite of or I'll feel sick. I think about how piggish I was before. What a difference a few pounds can make.

8/26/97

This morning Allen tries to talk to me, and asks, "don't you think you're crippling financially?" (in regards to wanting to move out) Oh, if he only knew! That's the part they can't see! I am crippling myself mentally, physically, and emotionally. Additionally, his claim that I live at home for free is false but they wouldn't understand that. I may not be paying with money but I'm paying at a greater cost with my health and well being. Nothing in life comes for free. **Nothing**.

8/27/97

It is Moving Day. Mom says I'm using her and Allen by moving. On the contrary, I'd be using them if I stayed. I don't want to depend on them or be stuck in a dependent situation. She is not happy either way.

Since she was so bent on that, I flipped it around in terms that she might understand. If I stayed home, I could save so much more money to get out to California, but I'm not. What does that say?

She responded, "oh, we're such mean, horrible people". I paused a beat and said, "frankly, yes you are". It felt *so* good to get that out.

9/2/97

It is approaching the time when I should call Mom to tell

her my information. However, I don't feel like I really want to. It's common courtesy, yes, but how has she displayed that to me? I cannot pretend that her words have not changed how I feel. I literally feel emptiness for her. She has alienated me so much. I don't feel anger, not even sadness, perhaps numb. I don't want her negativity and cruelty to seep in and corrode my new environment. It is precious and special to me and I will not hand her that power. Why should I go back to her?

    This is the end of my being dutiful daughter. It is not my duty. If I want to completely let go, that is my choice. It does not make me a mean, bad, or selfish person. You have endured enough cruelty from them. The best thing you can do is to take care of yourself. Only you know what is in your best interest. You and God. Don't worry about what anyone else thinks!

    I have the courage to stand up and say, "I won't allow myself to be treated this way". It's ironic that I'm painted as a selfish and terrible person. Mom is the most selfish person I know. Everything out of her mouth is a criticism or blame. She is not generous because generosity doesn't ask for anything in return. Further, she doesn't say sorry or thank you. Perhaps, yes, when I literally give her something. But she doesn't say, thank you for being my daughter, or thank you for that gesture, or thank you for such a nice day. She can't go to that level because it's too deep. She would drown in whatever her fear is. I feel sorry because she must be so afraid, so unhappy, and she doesn't know how to rescue herself. She doesn't know that she holds the key. Or maybe she does but simply cannot use it. That is the worst; having the knowledge but not applying it. That statement seems ironic because it seems to speak to another time and place. It points to the theory that she may have known about the abuse but could not do anything. I think that really could be a possibility. If it's true, then she's still living a lie. She's a victim of her own lie. What she doesn't seem to grasp, is that I forgive her. I can only feel compassion for her disposition, but she cannot forgive herself.

Five-month gap due to lost material:

From September to December 1997, I remained estranged

Michelle Bahret

from my mother and family only seeing her on three occasions: at Chris's baby shower, Thanksgiving, and Christmas Eve. It was unbearably painful, and a situation I did not know how to recuperate. I could not find words to express the heavy burden that I felt. I felt that too much weight was on me to fix it. I was not careless. I cared very much. In a time when I could not speak, or even have contact, silence was my only way of coping.

My family received this silence as a continuance of my ungrateful, manipulative behavior. They did not stop to ponder what could have happened. They were so ensconced in their image of me as a bratty ungrateful princess, that it didn't occur to them that this wasn't just my problem. The whole family had a problem but I couldn't take it on by myself. I was seething in pain.

On Christmas Eve, I went home for the traditional Chinese dinner. I did not eat much. Nothing much was said. I had decided to spend Christmas with Cathy O. because it was too stressful to be with family on a holiday. I wanted to relax and feel good. This was my measure of self-care.

The tension, confusion, anger, and hurt all came to a mind-blowing explosive eruption on the following day when I went home to return the CD player I had borrowed. The confrontation began quickly, gathering speed and momentum. Kevin and Chris were there getting ready to leave. Kathy and her fiancé Peter were arriving. Kevin was still pissed at me dating way back to the summer argument we had. He was the bully, and to my shock, everyone else chimed in. I stood there in disbelief listening to the blistering assaults. I felt that sickening, sinking sensation again. This couldn't be real. What had initially been a problem between me and Mom had spread a rapid firestorm through the entire family. I was resentful that no one had minded their own business.

Of course my silence was interpreted as rebellious and uncaring. I couldn't speak with seven people hurling insults at me, people who are supposed to love me. This isn't love, this is throwing me out in the ring with oxen, and I have to save my ass.

Fuck you all for doing this to me! You beat me to a pulp. So what if I moved out? So what that I have a mind of my own? So what if I fuck up (in your opinion)? So what if I don't listen to you? Am I going to be a martyr because of it?

The most baffling and mind-boggling thing is that they don't see their own prophecy reflected back. Everything they're accusing me of is how they're acting towards me. I could be very unforgiving but I can only pray that one day there will be healing and reconciliation. I cannot solve this by myself.

Kevin asked me why I didn't just turn around and leave. I looked at his face, all contorted with hate and anger, and then looked around the room. There wasn't anything I could say that would shed understanding. They had just showed me the exact reason why I had separated myself from them. I turned around and walked out not knowing if this would permanently sever the family ties.

One week later I deposited a letter for each family member with no return address. Then I boarded a plane. The destination: Los Angeles, California.

During my first week back in California, I found the studio apartment I had dreamed of nestled in Laurel Canyon, a temp-perm job in Century City, and a 1985 Pontiac Sunbird convertible. I had arrived in town! Everything came together at lightening speed. This assured me that the universe was reinforcing that this was right for me. All I had to do was live my life and let the rest take care of itself. If only it had been that simple...

2/13/98

I met with Katie this morning to discuss my goals. We do this twice a year, and it's my favorite thing to do. I set goals for my professional, personal, and spiritual life. Katie encourages writing them down free-style twice to see what repeats itself. We review the goals at the end of the year.

Nearing the end of my list, it was apparent to Katie that recovery was not one of my goals. She said I looked really thin and asked if it were anorexia. I was surprised because everyone in class told me how great I looked. On the other hand, it was also my first night back.

I need help. I don't want to become sick. Kate asserted that it's harder the longer you keep battling it alone. You're not alone.

I was relieved but now I'm scared. I don't feel ready. I feel too fat. I look at myself and although I don't see the skinniness, I do see a lifeless figure. There's no life in my face.

2/16/98
My life is vapid right now. No feeling. The only feeling I have is sadness every once in a while.

I lay on the sofa all day. I watched a movie. I only went out to buy food and throw up. I want to get off the food and back into starvation. I hate how my body feels. I long for that emptiness that starvation brings. When you don't even feel hungry but you could keep going all day. I'm determined to start losing weight again. My weight keeps going up and down. Now I just want to keep it going down. I feel like I have nothing else to do. It is so hard to do anything. If I could just put all my energy into acting and studying, but even without thinking, I'm back into the food. I do senseless things.

2/17/98
I have to push myself out the door. It's not good to stay holed up in the apartment, no matter how adorable it is. No matter, I can't really enjoy my apartment until I have a life to live.

It's time to accept differences now than similarities. Sometimes, line of action is necessary in the moment but it doesn't have to be deemed forever. It's determining how badly you want it. First, determine what you want and then commit yourself to it.

It's all in your attitude. How you feel about yourself. Begin small. Take small steps towards big things.

I'm afraid to eat anything. Eating is automatically bad so I must throw up. Even if it's something good for me. Today, I digested a yogurt, 4 fat-free cookies, an energy bar, and a small plate of spaghetti. That's A LOT.

God, give me strength.

2/18/98
I'm inspired watching the ladies' figure skating in the Olympics. It's such drama! It's all about determination. What I hear over and over again is training, training, and more training. Timeless work. And just about everyone had some sort of obstacle to overcome. Some small and some large. It seems to

come with the territory.

Dreams do come true. You can be ordinary or choose to be extraordinary. You know you have it in you. You have the stuff of what it takes to be a star. Determination, sparkle, passion, etc. Moreover, you have angels by your side.

My greatest strength is matched by my greatest weakness. For all the strength I have is matched by the deepest fear. I have such a strong desire to reach towards success and this dark demon stands in my way. I feel so split. Isn't everyone like this though? Everyone has got fears. You're not alone in that.

I want to say, "fuck it". Down with the bastards! I want to eat. But I'm so afraid of my weight. Yet I know I can't have both. And I can't live with this and expect that I'll be happy and successful. It may not stop you from achieving success but will you be happy to enjoy it? When you're at an awards show, will you be able to cherish the moment? Or will you be worrying about what you look like and what you're going to eat and not eat?

I already don't like how I feel in class. Hey, I can be the thinnest person in class but I'm the most miserable. Don't envy me and don't envy skinny models. You of all people, Michelle, know that empty existence.

I feel like I've made this choice before. I said Fuck it! And look, I'm back in this spot again! Who's to say it won't happen again? When will it ever end? The answer is, you don't know. You don't know if it will happen again. Perhaps you need to be more honest. You need to be around more people. You have a BIG tendency to not let people in.

Remember where there is fear there is also joy. No one but an anorexic can know how good it feels to complete a snack or a meal (and keep it down) after having starved for so long.

2/19/98
I'm sitting in a chicken café on Santa Monica Blvd. It's rainy and cold. I thought maybe I'd like a little chicken and rice. Those are my two "safe" foods.

I've kind of felt warm and queasy all day. Now the sight of food makes me feel a little sick. I'm hoping I can pull through class tonight. I feel so terrible that I cannot put my best self forward!

2/21/98

I saw a woman today in the mall who was about 5'10" and must have weighed 85-pounds. She was grotesquely thin. It made my heart skip a little. When I see what real thinness is, I don't feel nearly as sick. I'm not as bad as this woman is. I thought, "oh my god, I don't want to go there! And then my next thought was, "I don't feel worthy of recovering". I'm not thin enough. I'll never be thin enough!

2/22/98

I ask myself, "how do I feel?" like Katie had suggested I do several times a day but I still feel no response. I'm so far gone, so detached, so removed. Something that was pointed out to me was my compassion. It's a gift, not a nemesis. I absorb everything. And I think the emotional risks I've taken have caused me to shut down.

I don't know how to function in class. You need to keep going back. It will sustain you. And one day you'll just explode on the scene and everyone will cheer. But most of all, you'll be cheering the loudest. I can't wait for the day when I'm all smiles again and bursting with happiness. I'll be free. Right now I'm in my cocoon waiting to become a butterfly.

2/24/98

I ask myself, "how do I feel?" and I'm still blank. I'm starting to dread class because I won't be able to do the exercises. I'll look more foolish with each passing week.

2/26/98

I feel like I'm all tangled up and the more I try to free myself, the worst it gets. The twine, rope, whatever, just gets tighter.

2/27/98

Class was extremely difficult to get through. Katie talked to me afterwards. It's a struggle to just show up. I didn't want to go to class. I'm aware that class is a strong point. I can't drop out. Katie asked me not to hide, to keep her informed, but I have to be the one to call her. It's true, she can't be my mother and remember to call me. "Michelle, did you do what you said you were going to do?" I'm not a child. I have to be responsible. I have to be brave in asking for help and not isolate.

Katie said I *am* successful and she has no doubt that I'll succeed in acting. The only one who has judgement is me. She said I *do* have everything and just because my eating disorder has popped up again does not diminish my success. It perhaps is up again because now I can really focus on it. I don't have family intruding.

I'm still trying to figure out a system to lose weight. I can still lose weight while trying to get better. Isn't it expected? It happens all the time.

Usually, I don't know how hungry I am until I eat. My stomach just comes alive and titillates for more food. It's difficult to wage off hunger pangs, so it's better just to skip a meal altogether.

I have to exercise to burn food off. Right now I'm eating so little that how can I really lose weight? There isn't really much to cut back on, so the only answer is to burn calories I'm actually not taking in. I know it's crazy. I actually need this comfort as I try to find a way of getting better. Just holding on a little longer.

I'm getting sick and tired of looking at myself both emotionally and physically. I can't stop examining myself in the mirror. This routine is really boring! I think it's sad that I'm home on a Friday night. I should be out having fun.

I'm tired of my illness, my seriousness, and myself. Even as a kid, I was so serious. I couldn't laugh at myself. I didn't know how to have fun. Both the child and the adult in me are hurting.

I don't want to focus on heavy things. I don't want to focus on the abuse, my feelings, eating, etc. I think the solution is in seeking lightness and simplicity of life. Such as learning to play, laugh, and engage in child play.

Go to a playground and watch children play. You can learn from them. Go to a toy store. Go to the beach with a pail and shovel. Plan special events for you to look forward to during the week. Remember how exciting it was when you were going somewhere on the weekend? Even anticipating a favorite meal. My favorites were spaghetti and pizza. I liked applesauce too. I loved mornings of pancakes and French toast. Roller-skating.

Bike riding. Remember when make-up was fun? Buy little notepads and stickers. Get the BIG crayons and color.

Go to the children's bookstore. Look up at the stars. Go to the zoo. See a jazz band. Listen to Blues music. Get a children's movie and watch that. The whole point is getting in touch with the child in you. I think if you become friends with her and listen to her, you'll finally have peace.

I think my whole illness is compounded on getting in touch with this child. I'm afraid of her. She knows the Truth and I'm afraid she will tell me. I don't know if I'm ready to hear it. I'm afraid that I'm going to remember the atrocity of what really happened. What exactly happened *to me*? How far did the abuse go? Was I raped? Wouldn't I remember?

I stay away from men and intimacy because it keeps me from knowing. Intimacy is too scary because it might trigger something. Is there some way I can have a dialogue with this child? My older self meets with my younger self.

It's very hard for me to make peace without knowing what happened. I feel like I can't move on until I *know*. I think I have tried to move on but the eating disorder always serves as a reminder that there's something amiss. What do I need to do? And how do I do it?

2/28/98

Talked about this inner child stuff with Katie. Her feedback to me was that she's literally producing a hunger strike to be heard. It may be scary to listen but she's a part of you. She needs your attention. Working with her will help you deal with this. Break the chain of abuse. Learn to parent your self. Don't become the parent you grew up with. You want to be in touch with your kids. You don't want to repeat the same patterns.

Another thing is dealing with this while it's private. It's so much harder when you have the press in your face every day. God, I have reservations about the class knowing, let alone the whole world!

3/3/98

I'm so tired. Tired of life. I just don't know when I'll feel "light" again; when life isn't dragging me down. I feel burdened.

When can I laugh, skip a beat, feel one on one with God? I know these things could be so much worse. I could be homeless, in jail, or *really* hungry. I could have no friends or relatives. I could be blind or crippled. How come it feels so bad?

I get mad at myself when I eat because no one has to know if I don't eat. It could be so easy. I'm alone now. No one is monitoring my every move.

Hunger is an inconvenience. It doesn't occur to me to eat, and when I eat, it doesn't occur to me to digest it. It's just not an option. Immediately, the choice is to not eat or eat and throw up.

I tried eating chicken and rice for lunch today. It was exactly what I was craving. And I did feel better. I felt my body awakening; like a wilting plant just perking up. Not to full bloom but just enough. Still, it was a little too much rice. Then as I was walking by the concessions, free samples distracted me. Then I had to throw up. My whole day was disrupted.

I wish I could eat normally. It doesn't even have to be a lot. But it feels so scary. I'm mad that my weight doesn't seem to reflect where I am. I still look fat.

3/5/98

Last night, as I was going to sleep, I broke down into choking sobs. I feel nothing for days and weeks at a time and then something like this makes me realize how much I have buried.

The darkness became scary. Everything took on a spooky luminance. I felt like a little girl afraid of the dark.

I feel all alone because I am. I've created a world of isolation but what makes it harder is that everything is new. I don't have people who know me. It's good because I *can* break away from old patterns. I don't want to become my story.

3/8/98

I can't even eat something good because that means good energy, soul energy, and my mind is clear to think and my body has access to feel. What am I so afraid to feel? Is there something I'm afraid to acknowledge?

Michelle Bahret

3/12/98

I hate it when I see people who are skinnier than me! I'm not that skinny. I want to lose more.

I didn't want to go to class. It's harder now because I feel like people will get frustrated with me. No one likes a sourpuss. I feel more alone when no one can understand how I feel. I don't want to have to admit to an eating disorder because I feel too fat.

3/13/98

I feel so angry and confused. I hated class tonight. I wasn't happy to be there and I wasn't any happier when I left. Katie asked if I were glad that I came and I was rather blunt for a change. I said no. She inquired if I got any value from watching the scene studies, and again, I said no. She told me it was one thing to hide in myself, but to detach from what's going on around me is my way of creating indifference; trying to convince myself I don't care when I really do.

I walked away feeling totally dejected and defeated. Tears of anger stung my eyes. I walked slowly to my car wondering what I was feeling. I felt isolated and alone. I felt like I wanted to die. It wasn't really a suicidal thought. I wouldn't ever do that. It was just a sense that I didn't want to deal anymore. And I really didn't want to go back to class.

I was mad at Katie. I was honest with how I felt and she didn't validate that. But maybe I was upset because she was seeing the truth. I'm building this wall of denial so that I can justify my isolation. I wanted to leave class tonight. I think I don't care. It's easier to be detached. It's easier not to get too close.

3/14/98

I healed one relationship. I finally talked with Kirk whom I blew up at a few weeks ago. It makes me feel better about him as a friend because he totally accepted me even though I must have hurt him with my lashing out. He didn't judge me or argue his defense. He understood.

Since our conversation, I'm confused about what he meant about "helping me". He said he wants to help. But when I call him it's not necessarily help I'm asking for. I'm just looking for companionship. How does he feel about that?

I visited with Jane this afternoon too whom I haven't seen for weeks. Her piece of advice to me was to pick one thing at a time to work on. Pick what you're afraid of and do that.

I can control my emotions. Acting is about control. If I'm angry, I don't have to reveal that it was about abuse or how I was treated at home. I can use a lesser extreme. I can also put something away for a while and deal with it another time.

3/15/98

I feel really ashamed about my place in class. Although no one has criticized me, I still feel it. I don't know if it's worth opening up. I don't know if I want these people to know me. I don't want to prove myself.

Maybe I should just focus on myself and what I want to work on. Try not to conquer class. Don't try and get people to like or accept you. That will come naturally as you open up with your work.

I talked to Mom. I called her. No reason. I just figured that maybe it was time. She seemed surprised to hear from me but I'm sure it made her happy. I was a little upset afterwards because I didn't know what I had just done. Did I lose control or gain control? It all depends on my attitude. I'll look at it as gaining control. It's one step towards getting things back together. I figured that maybe its time to just accept what might not change.

3/18/98

The cupboard is bare and I don't know when I'll have money again.

3/19/98

Tonight I am going ahead with a monologue even though I don't feel ready. It doesn't have to be perfect. The point is, I need to break down my barriers, and part of that is risking vulnerability. I will allow myself to not be perfect. My classmates will not judge me. They will be glad to see me up there.

3/20/98

I forget how much I like going to the movies. I like how a film can change your perspective; how I'm a different person from when I walked into the theatre. I want to do better. I want to expand.

3/21/98

It's weird but when I realized that class was canceled for another three weeks, I had this sobering thought: what if I was to die while Katie was away? No one would know. A scary thought is that I wanted to get down to 88-pounds. I don't know how I arrived at that number. But it seems to indicate my feeling towards life. I seem intent on killing myself. Class will resume the day after my rent is due, and it appears that I can't handle either. That is my failure. What will I do?

3/22/98

I saw Sue, whom I haven't seen in a year, at Mev's party. She didn't even recognize me. I told her my hair was longer. But she exclaimed, "you're so thin, thin, thin!" She seemed honestly shocked. I stuttered until Jill finally said, "say thank you", and laughed. I did, but I don't know whether it was a compliment.

3/24/98

I experienced a miracle today. I had just recited the Serenity prayer when the phone immediately rang. I got an assignment. It's only for a day, but still, it's a job. Maybe it's the beginning of many more opportunities. I don't believe in coincidences. God answered my prayer.

At lunch I was looking around the cafeteria-observing people eating. I was sitting alone eating a cup of vegetables and I knew that wasn't quite normal. Some lunch items sounded lovely but sandwiches and pizza are no longer a part of my diet. Even a plateful of salad is scary to me. However, I want to be able to eat these things. I wonder how I got down to eating a cup of vegetables. BUT I was dipping them in real ranch dressing so I can't be a freak about food.

I was thinking about my relationship with food and I've concluded that it's not food I'm really afraid of. I'm just afraid to be full.

3/25/98
    I have $.30 cents to my name. I literally have nothing to eat. I have five cans of diet soda left. Oh, boo-hoo to me. Why should I feel pity?
    I called Rachel and it was sort of controlled and manipulative. I knew it was wrong to call her like this when she's 3,000 miles away.

3/29/98
    My former therapist called me at my request. Her suggestion is that I call Dad and then I apply for any job that I can. She said it would be hard but I need to ask for help.
    It's not the end of the world. I didn't commit a triple homicide. I acted on impulse and I made a mistake. Dad is the best person to go to since he has the least emotional baggage and involvement with me.
    I've been so focused on what their limitations are that I failed to see something very important. They still love me.
    The assumption is that they think I'm stronger than I look. When I get quiet and silent, they think I don't care but it's just the opposite. It just reinforces the whole twisted thing. In the midst of surrounding Mom, no one notices my own fragility. They must think I'm made of steel or something.
    Mom notices in me what she lacks- drive. I have the skills to pursue what I want and also the coping mechanisms. She never did and never will.
    The family situation just drove me over the edge. I was in a lot of pain and I fled. The worst outcome is that I go back east. I made a mistake and I have to deal with the consequences.

3/30/98
    I have the power to change my mind. Everything begins with my thoughts.

4/2/98
    I called Mev and told her the gravity of my situation. She asked me if I were suicidal. I didn't think so. I called all these phone numbers for emergency relief but because I wasn't planning to overdose right then and there, I wasn't deemed

serious enough to be helped. I don't have money. I don't have food. I don't have insurance. I feel too weak to hit the pavement and look for a job. I probably need to be on medication but I have nothing. I don't have money to put gas in my empty tank. Mev told me to hang on, that I would get through it. She went to the store for me and got food and gave me money for gas. I had never felt so touched and cared for by a friend. Mev is the most unconditional friend I've ever had. She just gives of herself and doesn't expect anything back. I could never repay her. She's very dear to me.

4/5/98

I finally got my house in order. I noticed that as I cleaned, my mental house also became less cluttered. I cried a couple times. I got overwhelmed but I did it. I eventually got things organized. It's tempting to throw things every which way but I kept conscious. It's the same with life. It's hard right now but I'll get through it.

The question that I kept asking myself was, "How?" How do I let go? How do I not let my family get to me? It's no use trying to translate them. They'll never understand.

This is the answer I got: the more I start to connect here and build my life, the less pain I will feel towards my family. I won't be as attached to it. The more I have going on, the less time I will have to think about it. It won't matter as much. Then eventually, they may not catch on, that indeed you are living your life and are happy. You're going to make it.

It feels like grief. I am mourning my family. Moving on and keeping busy are the cure. I can't control what they think or say but I can control what *I* think. I have to stop letting them get to me. Stop explaining yourself. You did nothing wrong!

4/5/98

I have no money and no food. This has happened three times this week. A church friend has invited me out to dinner. It's not a date. I wouldn't want it to be.

I'm going to enjoy dinner. I haven't had a good restaurant meal in so long. I'm going to eat protein. I'm not going to worry about my weight.

Counting Bones

I didn't weigh myself this morning. I got a big surprise yesterday: my period. I was horrified to see it because (1) it was early and (2) goddamn, why am I getting it? How little do I have to weigh to stop having it? I've been fluctuating between 101-103 pounds. It pissed me off.

4/6/98

Even though I'm starving and hungry, I'm afraid of my weight. I know inevitably that I've gained. And although I was still full from last night's dinner, I still ate because I think it's a blessing. I can't pass on food that is provided for. I know that is God.

I also realize two things. My perception of food is off and my stomach's capacity for food is small; which means that I'm still eating far less than what is normal, and I fill up faster, and stay full longer.

As soon as I cut back on food, my weight will drop again. And since my body is working over-time to digest, that in turn speeds up my metabolism. It's the opposite of dieters breaking a diet. You break the diet and you gain weight. I try eating again, but as soon as I stop, I lose weight. It's reverse action.

4/9/98

I finally saw Kirk in person. He came over to hug me. I can't totally remember what he felt like, but it was a soft feeling. He said, "you got skinny!" I shrugged it off. He touched my arm too, kind of gauging how thin it was.

We exchanged small talk. We're both keeping an eye out for each other. A couple of days later, we saw each other again, and I was able to ask about what was up for him. I sensed that he was at a crossroad. He agreed but he's keeping at it. I wanted to reach out and touch him but resisted. It didn't matter. He reached out for a hug. I hope my hug expressed what I couldn't say. I care.

A guy at church is smitten with me. On paper, I'm everything he's looking for. The problem is, I don't feel the same way. It makes me uncomfortable. He's too intense. I don't even feel comfortable writing about it. I hope this isn't how I make Kirk feel. However, it seems completely different to me. First, we're good friends. Second, the gender is opposite. Finally, we have a history with each other. He's never expressed feeling uncomfortable and Kirk is pretty open and honest. If he were uncomfortable, he wouldn't want to be touched by me at all.

I met with Katie. The remainder of this year will be about getting my health back. Seeking a relationship with my body, meeting people, and developing a support system. Being alone is not good for you right now. You have too much freedom to isolate and self-destruct.

4/17/98

I feel so amazingly good but nothing has really changed in my life. I must be surrounded with good energy. A lot of prayers must have been said for me. I just feel like God is with me and things are going to be okay. How different this was from a few weeks ago.

I talked to Cathy O. about the guy smitten with me and she told me to stay away from him. I knew my instinct was right. She said he's a con-artist. He doesn't listen and he likes to change people. He pretends to help people and uses God's name. He might really believe he's doing God's will but there's always something in it for him.

Even when I've made it clear to him that I'm not interested, he continues to make suggestive comments. He comes on too strong. I don't like it. This isn't about me; it's about him and how he's acting.

Through this experience, I am reminded that I can always count on my gut feeling to know what feels right. This guy was bad news. I know whom I like and don't like. I know who I am. My relationship with God is my own. Don't let anyone step over you like that.

For one month, I am practicing a prosperity plan through The Abundance Book by John Randolph Price. It is a birthday gift from Katie. This day I renounce my so-called humanhood and claim my divine inheritance as a Be-ing of God. This day I acknowledge God and only God as my substance, my supply, and my support.

During meditation, REALITY seemed to jump out at me. I've "cashed in" to false beliefs about myself that I've heard from family or unmeaning friends. This has left me feeling empty, impoverished, and believing in lack.

God is INSIDE me. He is not separate from me. If his prosperity is realized through me then I AM God and God is me. It's a partnership. I AM lavish, unfailing abundance.

It's like being a light beam. Increasing the wattage according to intensity. Some people shine very bright while others have little or no light at all. They don't realize they have the power within. You can turn on the switch. It's that easy. SIMPLE, it's really simple but we make it so difficult.

The reality of me is that I am a Be-ing of God. CHOICE is an operative word. I choose my thoughts and beliefs.

4/18/98

My body is just an outer shell of my mortality. But deep in spirit, mind, and soul, I AM divine. I can break free from mortal conditions if I remember that I have, am, and always will be a divine being.

I feel like this body is so limited and contained. My spiritual self is so much bigger, way bigger. I don't have to let my body constrict me.

4/19/98

I am not separate from Abundance. I am not separate from God. It's all inside me. I can choose to embrace the light. I don't have a very far place to go to seek the light of truth.

My mind is infinite. It knows no bounds or limitations. *I* have posed those limits. My abundance becomes visible as I become aware of this. The light will get brighter and brighter, and therefore, attract people who are warm, caring, and want to share. Happiness, peace, and serenity will be your abundance. It is not just money that amounts to wealth.

I'm tired of this fucking disease! I have to say goodbye to it. How much longer can I really endure? I haven't reached the complete point of hatred. I don't hate it enough. It still works for me. But it's all a big lie.

My thoughts turned to recovery. That God within me is the same supply I can draw upon for strength to face my battle with food. I can sit down and eat. I can invite Jesus to my table. I'm not alone. I can picture rubbing anointment oil all over my body and letting it sooth and heal me.

5/2/98
    I felt new moments of despair tonight. I feel like dying. I've put this weight on myself. God wants me to have this dream but I'm the one who creates the expectation.
    All I wanted was to go back to the day when Mom would bring me Jell-O or toast when I was sick in bed. That was when she was most useful in motherhood. That was the only time we connected. And now I'm sick and I only want her to love me like that again. Of course a few days of TLC does not cure anorexia. So I have to turn it around and let myself be the mom. I'll take care of the child that feels lost and scared.
    I really feel like I won't rise above it. Each time I fall, I fall further down. I stare into my plate of food and how my life has been sucked into a vacuum. And I don't feel ready to let it go.
    I have moments of great strength. It's hard to believe that just a week ago I stood strong and centered during my one-word piece monologue. I orchestrated my story into class and it was so empowering. Now I don't feel strong. I feel like giving in.

5/4/98
    I hate life. I hate myself. I want to check out. How is that? Tomorrow I start my death sentence. I'm starving myself. I don't have courage to commit suicide but anorexia is a clever disguise.
    I don't want to be around anyone or anything. Forget making it as an actress. I don't think I'm making it in life.
    It has been five months since I came back to California. I haven't accomplished anything. Is this a question of geography? What am I doing?!?

5/6/98
    I feel like I'm teetering on a tight rope. I feel like I'm gaining weight and losing control. My clothes still fit but I feel bigger.
    I went to a workshop on eating disorders. I didn't really get anything out of it because it was very introductory. However, I may have gotten something self-destructive out of it. A large part of anorexia is a physical addiction to the release of endorphins.

Right now I'm not exercising. I've been starving and purging. But when exercise is combined with starvation, it increases the amount of endorphins, and weight loss is more rapid. I think I'll feel more in control if I exercise.

5/11/98
I feel so incredibly sad, frustrated, but more sad than anything. I don't know why. I don't think it has anything to do with my outer surroundings. It's something deep inside.

5/16/98
My outer surroundings are spinning wildly out of control. The good thing is that I'm finding some sort of connection. Jill is becoming a good ally. She's helped me so much. She's driven me around, she's gotten me a place to stay for a few days, and perhaps I'll get a job through the referrals she has. She at least understands how I feel. If I slip into depression, she doesn't tell me to be grateful. She understands.

A Return to the East Coast:
Being completely broken in spirit and, not only penniless, but also deep in debt, my family welcomes me home without question:

5/27/98
Wow, I'm back on the East Coast and I feel surprisingly good. I've never felt this here but I feel like I *am* home. I feel calm and safe. Both Mom and Allen have been extremely easy-going and nice and I don't think it's an unnatural thing. Mom said she was glad to have me back and Allen seems supportive. There's no resentment or tension and I don't even feel it bridging. I think there was a definite shift. I think Cailin has helped Mom tremendously. She is her joy. She has something to always look forward to now and to smile about.

Oddly enough it seems this is where I belong, with my family. For the time being. It's just so weird how my usual nervousness seems to be melting away. I really think things are going to be okay.

5/28/98

I appreciate birds' singing, the humming of a lawnmower, the perfect 80-degree sunshine. I love the full green heads of trees. I don't think I will miss LA this time. I think I have fallen out of love. I still want to act but LA itself is no longer the dream.

5/30/98

Something different is taking place. They're calm so I'm calm. I no longer feel this sense that the other shoe will drop. I'm not even doubtful that this is the "honeymoon" period. Maybe I should give into this trust that it CAN be this way all the time.

A part of me is delighting in the availability of food and another part is still living like it won't last. I'm still at war with starving, wanting food, and having it.

6/1/98

I threw up once today, and as I did, I thought, "there's no reason for me to do this". Everything is good. Nothing is wrong. There's no conflict, no yelling, and no tension. But I will definitely screw things up if I keep doing this!

I just realized that I've been in love with Kirk for two years. And I've been wondering why I've been hurting again. That's a mighty long time to feel for someone. It's going to take time to get over him.

6/7/98

It is mid-day on a cool and cloudy day. Enya's music is playing on the CD player. It's a good day to sit and write. I feel so vapid. I want to write and let everything flow out but I'm trying very hard to avoid it. I've been fidgeting all day. I'm restless. I've even placed judgement on what I write. Why don't I reflect on events, things I see or hear about? All I write about are my emotions, obsessions, and such self-absorbed, tedious things. It's so BORING! Like, get over yourself!

6/8/98

Yesterday I felt fear for my life and today I feel normal. Working today helped me to feel better. I was too busy to think. That is what the problem is. Thinking about it is depressing.

Counting Bones

Staying busy will alleviate it.

6/15/98

  Mom says I look thinner than I appeared when getting off the plane. This is hard to believe. I've been *struggling* with my weight. But she wouldn't believe me when I said I wasn't thinner. I don't have credibility on my side. Needless, to say, I don't want any arguments to start. To talk about it means to take accountability and I haven't decided that I want to deal with it. I'm not ready to gain weight and deal with those feelings.

6/17/98

  I had an emotional breakdown today. I talked out loud to God in tearful prayer. I don't know what my salvation is. What will bring me back from the edge? I'm not courageous. I'm not strong. I just want to be left alone. I want to die. And yet, that isn't even enough for me. That's not my wake-up call. If I talk to someone then that means I have to move forward. I'm not ready. I don't know if I can do it. I'm a burden. My weight isn't low enough. I already feel too fat. I feel like I'm bulging everywhere.

  I can't talk. I don't have the right to speak. Everything is twisted and upside down. It's like being inside a FUN HOUSE. I look in the mirror and I can't even recognize me. Who am I? Everyone has a perception. My whole family thinks I'm a liar and a thief. I'm sneaky and secretive. My desire for control and lack of trust, or much rather, absence of trust is what led me to cut myself off and wrack up bills. Just like my eating disorder, it's a false illusion that once I have this, this, and this, that I'll be okay. And I'll pay for it later.

  I've failed. I've failed as a daughter, sister, and friend. Everyone is disappointed in me. Everyone questions why I didn't pursue drama earlier, since I basically wasted my college degree. These are questions that I haunt myself with; to hear my insecurities spoken out loud only seems to confirm my failure even more.

  I don't feel like I have options. I'm a deadbeat. The only thing I'm good at is losing weight. Being thin. Getting thin. Recovery didn't get me anywhere. I feel like I am literally trying to carve out my body to reach my spirit. I'm a spiritual being inside a human shell. This shell is too burdensome. I don't belong. I long for a place to be free, to feel free. Can't I ask God to set me free?

Anorexia is a disguise for suicide. If I slashed my wrists or overdosed, that would be blatant, but complications from this disease...it's more complex. No one sets out to say, "I'll commit suicide by starving myself". Even with this, I haven't any courage. I've failed at having an eating disorder.

I think about my family. They never knew me. Who am I anyway? Shall I plunge downward in that dark spiral never to resurface? Or do I decide to have a place in the world? I have to feel better by getting thinner. That's the only measure of which I feel good. I want to chisel at my body like an artist. I want to see my bones in pure form. I want to know how it feels. I don't want to need anyone.

On financial debt:
6/18/98

Debt is a good way to remain dependent. It's another way to be heard, for everyone to fuss over you, but it's not the answer. For you, even if it's negative, it affirms the only way you know how to be loved. You never got emotional love, so you reached for a place that you knew would hit a nerve in the family central system.

6/22/98

I spent the afternoon at Karen's house. I shared my writing with her. I think I wanted someone in the family to know who I was and I elected her. She said she felt honored for my sharing with her. But even though she told me not to worry, I can't help but wonder if I did the wrong thing. I have so long believed myself to be a burden.

6/23/98

For uncertain reasons, my period fills me with self-loathing. I hate it. It has always been my goal to lose it, and I never have.

I've made it a mission to stop throwing up. Bulimia is so unpure, unsophisticated, and undisciplined. I don't want involvement with food. I've gotten to a certain point with my weight, but I know that if I want to lose more, then I have to stop being a bulimic.

6/27/98
 I wish I could find tricks to disguise not eating. To me, it doesn't make sense to push food around a plate. It NEVER looks like you're eating! I take very small bites or put the bare fork in my mouth and hope no one notices. I spit food out into my napkin, but I can't get away with that too many times. There has to be a way where I can knock food onto my napkin on my lap. It's tricky and I already can see they've picked up that I haven't been eating. That's why I have to be more selective and exercise to make up for what I *am* eating.
 I hate the fact that my days seem to always be revolved around food, my weight, and what I look like. My life is one-dimensional. I look at other people who seem happy and well rounded and I want what they have. I feel a stab of sadness. It can't be nostalgia because I've never had it. But I have something they don't. I'm skinny. I don't know why that has such importance. I *do* judge how other people look. I hate it when there are people skinnier than I am, especially if they're "normal". I feel better when I'm thinner and yet I know I'm really sick to judge people for that. I don't have a life when they do. I'm afraid. If I could get better without gaining weight, I would. But gaining weight means needing more, feeling more, living LARGE. It seems I am trying to suppress every appetite that I have. I'm putting my life into one simple box. The mother in me is pretty annoyed and frustrated that I cannot control this child. The war at hand is my ignorance of her. When I picture her I just see her as whining with a tear-stained face. It's pretty horrifying that rather than feel compassion, I only feel indignant and angry by her needs. I just want her to SHUT UP! I guess that's where the hunger strike comes in.

6/29/98
 Diary entries reveal what's going on in someone's head at the moment. Oprah always asks this question to an eating disordered individual: "what's going on inside your head?" The obsessive thinking and rituals paralleled with the insights and breakthroughs of recovery can make for compelling reading.
 Over the years, as I wrote, there were times I really felt like

Michelle Bahret

I was writing for someone else's eyes; that it could be read one day. I've never written for anyone but myself, but some of the things I have written could make a difference, from having been in the eating disorder to the other side of it.

In high school it still seemed to be an experiment. I was in the hospital once for anorexia and bulimia but then it seemed to dissipate. It was a mistake to think I had overcome it, because in hindsight, it was beginning to build and take momentum. It was the "eye of the storm" so-to-speak. By the time I reached college, all hell broke loose and the "storm" unleashed its fury.

I remember during my first hospitalization, at 16, writing my first piece of work although I wasn't aware of it. It was the hospital staff that first recognized me as a "beautiful writer". I had to write about my feelings after not being able to complete my meal. All I remember is writing about how there was too much bread. How poetic can that be? I was astonished to be complimented on my writing.

On the high school experience:
6/30/98

I'd want to go back and do all the things I didn't do. I'd want to seek out all the people I didn't talk to. Now I understand that I was TOTALLY unapproachable.

Isn't it better to risk everything? It hurts more to live inside out. I would like to be known for being honest, truthful, elegant, and pure goodness. I want people to know how I feel about them to ensure that there is never a question. And when I feel my emotions I want to embrace them full-heartily and discard the ones that cause self-destruction. Emotions aren't bad, only how we choose to act.

An eating disorder is mainly unexpressed emotion eating away at the body (my words).

Synapses of an Eating Disorder

Pasty skin shriveling inward
Cracked lips, haunted smile
Glass-like eyes, pretty doll

Counting Bones

Protruding bones to cushion fall
Walking, slow motion, this baby crawls
The world silently goes by

    I threw up 5x today. It's been a long time since I've had such a day. There were several thunderstorms and torrential downpours. I loved it. It got so dark outside. It lent to a warm and cozy feeling inside. On such days I like to cook and bake. I made brownies and popcorn and threw up. I had cheese and crackers, buttered toast, pasta and threw up. Five candy bars and potato chips. Threw up. More brownies, marshmallow and peanut butter with graham crackers. Threw up. In the midst of all this, I cleaned the refrigerator and bathroom spotlessly.

    I don't know what to do. I feel like my life is dwindling away. I have to be really careful with what I decide. I don't know anymore what God wants me to do. Am I fulfilling my purpose? Where am I supposed to go next? Should I keep acting? What about writing? I feel like I don't have any time to spare. In fact, it feels too late. Whatever I was going to do, I should have done ten years ago.

7/3/98

    It is strange how just last week I was obsessed with food all day long and now it doesn't occur to me that I haven't eaten breakfast, don't intend to have lunch, and eat the smallest amount of dinner I can get away with.

    I baked some cookies today and even sampling a small bite of batter made me feel sick; too rich. I like this phase of not eating much better than the constant bingeing and purging. I feel more in control and energetic. I don't think about food unless I eat it.

    My feelings about food gatherings are different too. It used to stress me out tremendously but now it doesn't affect me. I just pick at it. It worries me a little getting through this week. My solution is to only eat when people are around, when it's absolutely inescapable. That way I still have control. There is no way I am going to get stuck with eating too much. I'm NOT going to gain any weight. I'm going to keep losing. Nothing is going to ruin my progress.

I felt some sadness when Kathy and Chris were talking about Dad's reaction to Kevin's new fatherhood and 30th birthday. It was the first time he sent Kevin a sentimental card. Kathy also experienced this sentiment on her wedding day. Kathy says he never reveals his emotions; only at hallmark moments in life. I can't recall a time when Dad has gotten choked up over me. I have not reached any hallmark moment and I don't know when, or if, I ever will. I'm trying to find my way. I pray that I will. I feel like I'm just floundering with no sense of direction.

7/7/98
I haven't talked to any of my California friends because I do feel like I've failed and it's too painful to speak. I don't want to say to Kate that I haven't gotten help. I don't want to talk to anyone.

It's weird because I don't see it. I'm normal thin. I don't see bones sticking out. Plus, since no one says anything to me, it just makes it seem more normal. If I could just stop the bulimia for strictly starvation, then there would be no problem. The weekend threw me off course. My appetite got wet. Purging redeemed me. I did not eat breakfast, lunch or dinner, just a handful of candy.

I don't know how much my mistakes cost me. If I had been more patient, I would have gone to California with my own money and confidence. Perhaps I would have reconciled with my family, gotten help, and then I wouldn't have been such a mess. But maybe this transition with family wouldn't have happened if you hadn't acted so drastically. Yet, now that you're back, you're not any closer to getting help or resolving your problem. You're headed in a downward spiral. You know where you're going and you don't want to talk to anyone because, essentially, you don't want to be stopped. It's like suicide for you.

I don't know how much time I chopped off by making the wrong choices. I can imagine seeing my life before me and seeing what could have been. I am so mixed up! I can no longer make sense of my life and what I'm doing.

I feel like I need a spiritual guide.

On the realization of a dream based in vain:
If I act from pure fun and enjoyment then it doesn't matter

whether I become famous or not. I'm going to do it anyway, and I'll still be the same person no matter which way it goes. However, if you're waiting to be famous to *be* someone then you're going to be sadly disappointed, and you will never have fun. You won't know how to have fun because you'll always be trying to uphold the image of what you imagined yourself to be. You have to be comfortable with who you are right now.

I'm not a cutthroat person and Hollywood is a cutthroat environment. I don't want to read between the lines. I want to know what people are *really* saying. I want to know who people *are*.

7/8/98

I just want to turn away and focus more and more on starving myself and losing more weight. I only get so low and then I put some back. I want to push further and go where I've never been. It's just a satisfaction quencher.

7/9/98

I don't know what I'm worth to anyone. I don't know if it's imagined or just how I feel. I want to draw away more because of the shame I feel, only to fuel the isolation more so. A part of me feels like throwing in the towel. Let's do everything I'm afraid of; the opposite of what I'm doing now.

I'm tired of living my life day to day ruled by thoughts of food and weight. Worrying about how much I'm eating, how much I'll gain, and constantly checking the mirror. I never give up because I'm never good enough. I couldn't be the best.

For the choice of Recovery:
7/11/98

In order to make things happen for myself, in order to turn things around, and not let anyone or anything get to me, I have to be over-brimming with love. When you love and feel good about yourself, there are no ailments. With love there is no fear. When you love your body, you can love *all* body types. You won't miss what you used to look like or feel jealous towards the 5% of the population that is genetically thin.

You won't be broke because you'll believe you deserve

enough and more. You're not attached to money, making it freer to flow and circulate. You won't attract unhealthy people because love attracts love. You won't make bad choices or judgement calls because you'll trust your own instinct.

I have to get out of my head! I have to stop believing these fallacies about myself. It doesn't matter what I've done. I'm worthwhile and I'm ENOUGH. I deserve to eat. I deserve to live. I deserve to have fun.

The fight to Believe continues:
7/12/98

I want to change how I think and feel. I'm not living consciously. Most of the time I'm just afraid or numb. Those are my two feelings.

I don't want to coast through life. I want to be fulfilled. I haven't had an appreciation for waking up and having another day for a long, long time. I don't pay attention. Everything is just mindless. Wouldn't it be something to approach each day with wonder? To anticipate eagerly what the day will bring? I want to be enthused and awe-struck. I wouldn't even think of giving thanks for the food that I eat.

I feel that I'm just hanging in mid-air, and any minute, I could drop. I feel weightless in the sense that I don't feel grounded. I can't grasp onto anything. I have to get out of myself. I have to get out in the world.

7/14/98

Today was one of my happier days in quite some time. It began with hearing about a nation-wide search by NBC Daytime Programming. It is at the Galleria tomorrow. I'm working half a day and then I'm going.

I just think it would be so ironic if I got discovered here, after everything I've been through. What a story that would make! I would be coming full circle with NBC back to the days of my internship. What great fun it would be to meet with my talent managers, and say, "Remember me?"

I'm not thinking about being disappointed. I have a better chance than if I didn't go. But perhaps more important is how I feel now. I've been happy and excited all day. That means a whole lot. I must pay attention to that. When doubt sets in, this will be a reminder to me that, this *is* the life I want to pursue, and it **will** happen. You have to pay attention to what excites you because that is where your passion resides.

7/15/98
Okay, I didn't get selected to read, and I did feel disappointed. I was so sure that they were going to like me enough, to have me read for them, but no one in my group was picked.

I can't get into this dejection mode: "well, maybe if I wore my hair curly, or I was in a different group, or I wore something different..." Get used to this, Michelle. It doesn't mean anything. They obviously had a type they were looking for and you weren't it. It doesn't mean you won't get picked for anything else. But do feel good for having tried. And keep trying! Some day this will be a fond recollection. All the actors, who are currently working, have been rejected along the way, but they kept going.

7/16/98
My thoughts during lunch break (I didn't eat) are that it seems like anorexia is my career. It's what I'm good at. I'm losing weight, consuming 1300 calories, which is not exactly at starvation level. I'm thin bordering on emaciation. I have warranted attention for being thin, though it hasn't always been welcomed. Mostly, it's embarrassing, and yet I feel like I've lost something by giving it up. It's painful to be "normal", to no longer have people look at me with wistful or envious glances. I have not reached a point where people would deem me pitiful. I have kept myself neatly in the middle. I'm not normal-thin but not scary-thin either, just enough to cause "concern".

I want to be seen and not seen. I want to quietly escape out the side door and wonder when my absence will be noticed. I watch people fuss over me with a mixture of fascination and dismay. I don't speak because no one understands my language. My body has its own language but they don't understand that either.

I want to feel like I have a right to be here.

Michelle Bahret

Struggling to understand an unresponsive friend:
7/16/98
Has the time come to move on? Is it time for new friends? Why have all my closest friends drifted away?

7/18/98
I have a problem with expectations. I'm co-dependent in friendships. I have one-way relationships where I give more. I do all the calling. Otherwise, the relationships wouldn't sustain themselves. Although I know I should stop, I still want to call.

It's taking care of you. It's saying, "I care about myself and I deserve to be given thought and consideration." It's time to start cleaning out. Create anew, out with the old, in with the new.

7/20/98
I feel depressed about depletion. No money. No stimulation at home. I'm forever sick of looking for items Mom has misplaced. While I was away for the weekend, she was mad most of that time, thinking I had taken some of her stuff. I didn't.

I hate how no one talks here. I'm struck again by how little Mom knows about me. However, she didn't even seem interested. She never asks me any questions. I know I should turn this around and begin the process myself but I feel so daunted by it. It's easier just to share my life with people who are interested and want to listen. They ask questions. It's a two-way thing.

Over the weekend, I got a few comments about being thin or being teased because I had special requests. I didn't talk about it because I didn't want to draw attention to myself. There's a thin-ism in society too. People think it's okay to comment on being thin, unaware that it can be a hurtful and invasive thing. They automatically assume that you'll gloat from the attention, but most often, it's annoying. Especially when I know that, with me, I've done terrible things to my body. However, I can imagine how most "skinny" people feel. No one would ever say,"oh, you're so fat". They'd whisper it behind your back. But being thin is so upheld by society, and discussions of diet so common amongst women, that there are no boundaries.

No matter how thin I get, my bones are just too big to

achieve that stick figure. I'll always have hips, thighs, and a butt. Yet I don't want to get any bigger because I hate those body parts. I haven't gotten my period yet and I pray that I don't. That sounds weird when most women would be concerned. I've just never been interested in my period. For once, I'd like to be without it.

7/21/98

Last night I had an emotional breakdown. The dam burst loose and Mom and Allen saw what I've done so often in private: sob uncontrollably. I told Mom that I was scared because I wanted to die. The temptation to swallow a bottle of pills was so great and it wasn't what I wanted. I just had no idea what to do.

Maybe this is what it takes to move forward; the realization that I can no longer cope. Today was a little better but what about the next time I crumble in despair? Those days are becoming more frequent. I don't know how many more of those days I can survive. When you're crazed in those pivotal moments, you don't have the rationality to think clearly. You can act out of character and do things you wouldn't normally do. Either this disease is going to kill me or I'm going to kill myself. That's the bottom line.

7/23/98

I had a moment of despair last night. Just looking at myself in the mirror, fixated on my collarbones and chest for a few minutes, produced a rising sadness that flowed out through tears.

I felt like I needed to get to a place to speak to God. Somewhere vast like the ocean or a big church. But then I thought, "HE'S HERE." I don't have to go anywhere. I listened to the sounds. Birds singing, an airplane, cars going by. I stared at the plants on the ground, the bark of the trees, an ant crawling by. And I thought, "How do I close this gap between what I want to do and what is reality? How do I find my place in the world? How do I learn to be okay AS IS?" I've already got a place just by being ME!

I can only understand things in relation to bones; the outline of my ribcage, collarbones, hipbones... The way I stand in the light and shadows all make it appear a little different. I create my own artwork. Sculpturing my body, chiseling away at the flesh and bone. But I'll never have a masterpiece. Pretty soon, the canvas hardens, becomes barren and stone. It cracks and it crumbles. No more Michelle left.

I believe I still have a talent for acting and writing. But something much larger was luring me and stampeded my growth. The pursuit of stardom, being important, making a difference overshadowed the real work of art itself. Rather than letting nature take its course, I bulldozed my way to the top and didn't get very far. It's because I'm focused on exterior things rather than the interior. Don't let fame be the absolute. Let it be a by-product of what you love to do. Remember that you're already a star! So let that star shine through.

7/23/98

I could almost see straight lines in the mirror. I like being completely flat when I turn sideways.

7/24/98

I feel ashamed to show my body. It's hard because it's not so easy to cover up in the summer. I've been curious about the party tomorrow but I don't want to wear a bathing suit. I don't want to be tempted by food though I have felt strangely detached from it. Moreover, I can't deal with people's questioning glances or comments. I don't want to explain why I'm not eating or why I'm thin. And although I like Colin (a guy I had met at my cousin's party), I'm not sure if I want to go out with him. Any other time I might have been stronger. I don't want to feel. I don't want to fall in love, if that should happen. It's losing control. You have no control over something like that. And I don't want him to know about me.

I'm not physically attracted. He's nice to talk to but I don't get that feeling inside like I did with Kirk. Maybe it takes time. I just wish it could happen mentally. I can't stand feeling one way before the other. However, I know a big part of all this, is just me shutting down and wanting to be left alone. I have an image of me pulling down the shades and putting up a sign: Relocated. Date of Return undetermined.

7/26/98

For the first time I can actually feel my body eating away at itself. I can feel the skin stretching over the bone. I can see the point where the flesh becomes hollow. My face looks a little haunted with sunken eyes, pointed chin, and hollow cheeks. My stomach and buttocks have been sore and it's not from doing back-kicks or sit-ups.

Romantic Philosophy:
I have to know a guy first before becoming romantic. It doesn't make sense to me to be romantic first and get to know second. Holding hands or kissing someone does not make me feel good if I don't have a feeling about that person yet. I wouldn't expect these gestures to produce the feeling for me.

Mother-May-I?
She's worried about me being too disclosing with people, especially when meeting new ones. I don't know how she imagines me. It takes me a great deal to trust someone enough to tell him or her about myself, and when I do, it is for a good reason only.

7/28/98
OK. I'm beginning to think that I have to *gain* weight. I'm becoming more self-conscious of how I look. It's strange how I'm afraid to show my body just as much as an overweight person would be. Or anyone for that matter. It's not my body causing pain, though I want to believe it is.

I have to think about how I feel right now. I haven't eaten for days. Throwing up cancels out everything. No breakfast, lunch, or dinner. Not even a snack. I don't even think about eating. I have no concept of time either. Mealtime goes by without me taking much notice.

I don't ever remember it being like this. It never got this extreme. I never was oblivious to time or meals. The phrase "I'll never eat again" rings true here. These days, alone, I've taken advantage of not eating. And when I've eaten politely in front of others, I've been able to throw up in time. It's not an option to keep it down. I have no intention of eating.

It used to alarm me hearing these extreme starvation diets of anorexics, like one teaspoon of yogurt for breakfast and a handful of grapes for dinner. I never saw myself getting like that.

The only thing I allowed myself today was one shredded wheat biscuit. That's 36 calories. Yet I never set out to accomplish that. It just proceeded that way.

8/1/98
I think I write about the food, not only because I'm consumed by it, but also because I want to remember what this feels like. I told myself that this is the worst I've ever felt. Each time my world gets a little bit darker, a little more obsessive, and a bit more abstract.

All my thoughts are consumed by food, hunger, weight, and what I look like, etc. I can't write. I can't think. I can't enjoy what I'm doing. Most of the time I want to sleep because I'm so tired and weak. I know my face must look pasty and wan to on-lookers. My speech is slow. I'm always hungry. I'm either not eating or eating and puking it up. Everything looks good. I still have a distant memory that if I just eat what I want, I won't crave every food on the planet. Half the stuff I'm eating wouldn't even appeal to me. One or two bites of food tastes much better than eating the whole thing and heaving it.

I haven't been able to talk to God. This feels like Satan to me.

8/5/98
Apparently, my body doesn't reflect any sign of distress. Nothing came up in my blood or urine samples. The doctor said I was OK. A part of me feels like "okay then, no problem". There is no crisis.

I'm in a tug of war now. It would be so easy to forego recovery when everything is in the norm. I'm not in medical danger.

8/7/98
This eating disorder poses many paradoxes. I want to be around people but not for too long. I hate being alone and yet I feel boxed in. I want to be strong, open, and free. However, I'm weak, closed off and trapped. All the things you imagine "thin" are ethereal. I weigh 99 pounds and I still feel fat. I still want to lose more weight. Because I still have legs and arms. I'm not

supposed to have a body. And I'm curious as to how chiseled I can get.

It was interesting looking over my medical records. In retrospect I had all the ingredients for the recipe of an eating disorder. As a 4 year-old I already displayed perfectionist attitudes. I already worried about my performance.

This was before the sexual abuse. My personality traits were already established. It's unfortunate that the abuse compounded to it.

8/10/98

OH MY GOD! My weight jacked up to 103 pounds over the weekend. How did that happen? Yes, I ate a little more, but not enough to put on 4 huge, ugly pounds. It makes all the difference in the world, how I feel, and what I see.

Got to get it off pronto! Maybe it will go away just as fast as it came on.

Been fighting the compulsion to take laxatives. Just looking at the box in the store caused me to have nausea. They make me want to gag. Laxatives scare me. I swore I'd never use them again. My last experience with them, I was convinced I was going to die if I succumbed into unconsciousness. I never want to feel that fright again. Even if it means sacrificing a sure 5-pound weight loss. It's not worth it.

It's a bit difficult to ponder letting go of the dream. I thought I was always worldly; that a small town was too constrictive. I thought I'd be restless and unhappy. But going to LA didn't produce any answers.

It seems to me that I could never get started. If this is what I loved to do, then I would think I'd thrive, but I began to die.

I liked the idea of jet setting and traveling from movie shoots. I liked the idea of being famous with a story of inspiration and hope. I liked the idea of being financially well off and uninhibited. But I'm not so sure if I agree with the lifestyle. I don't want to be a part of it, and when I am, to fight it. I don't like the business and it's a very hard business.

I just think pursuing acting cost me more pain than joy. Although I experienced many wonderful moments, I'm not fit to be tied. I don't think I could be in Hollywood and be healthy at the same time. All of the ideals there just feed into all of my neuroses. I never got to the starting line- and look how sick I was.

I don't think I could enjoy being famous or would want to inherit that lifestyle. So much goes into "making it" but what about afterwards? Once you're famous, you can never go back to non-famous. Your life changes forever.

There will be some people who will be disappointed by your change of heart. There are people who want to have the credit of saying "I knew her when" but that's the wrong reason to be big and famous. Professionally speaking, I'll never know how far my talent could have gone. I like acting but I don't like the industry.

The way I see it is that God *does* work in mysterious ways. If I'm meant to do this, I'm sure he'll find a way to bring me back to it. But I don't want to seek it anymore. Let it seek me if it wants to because I just can't put in the effort and smarminess that is required of me to make it in Hollywood. I'll be one of those people who "fell into it". I know it sounds naïve but that's where I stand now. And I'm okay with it.

I want to be open to God and his direction. Faith is opposite of fear. The eating disorder is like the devil and how I feel is like hell. When I feel grief about eating or my weight going up, is when I need to pray. All those thoughts in my head telling me I'm fat and can't eat are the devils. I want to change my focus on food to a spiritual substance. It brings back respect for food and becomes nourishing and healing. When you're intact spiritually, you automatically want to treat your body well by eating right and keeping in shape. Balance and moderation in all things.

Eating Disorders and Christianity:
8/11/98

Food plays a big part of Christianity. The one thing I want to control is what God is in control of. The Last Supper and Eucharist order us to eat. The body is very sacred. Jesus says, "take this (bread) and eat it."

You're not alone in faith. Even before you pray or think of God, God has planted this desire in you. He wants to hear from you and he wants to respond.

I've been feeling very bad for 14 years. I can't really

remember the last time I felt good with the exception of college graduation. I didn't have fun in high school or college. Nor did I frequent the dating scene. This was not by conscious decision. While everyone else was relaxing and having their fun, I spent my school vacations in and out of treatment centers. It's time to start feeling better!

8/12/98

I've started taking an anti-depressant. I took it before eating to make sure I don't throw up. It worked.

When I think about my body changing and ceasing to purge, I comfort myself with knowing that beauty equals self love. When you feel good about yourself then you'll automatically feel good about your body. Even on wistful days, your new strength will help you cope. Everyone feels kind of crummy once in a while. On those days you'll treat your body with extra care.

When you feel good, you won't want to purge. It may not go away but you'll be able to fight it. You'll be able to see the danger in it. It **always, always** progresses if you don't stop it right away. It's best just not to do it at all. I know I can do it. I CAN do it.

8/17/98

I'm sick of talking about food. I'm aware that I can't seem to do anything else. I don't care about much. However, I have wistful thoughts that seem to inquire of my desires.

All I want is to enjoy nice things and being with good company. I don't want to be extravagant but I want to have the freedom of indulging; that if I see something unique, I don't have to feel guilty buying it. I want to be able to travel, have little weekend get-aways to charming bed & breakfasts. Places that are quaint with friendly people, lots of trees, and natural scenery.

I want to have someone, a companion, to share these things with. I want to feel serene and peaceful. I want to feel comfortable and beautiful within my own skin. I thought being thin would help me feel this way. It didn't. I only feel more disillusioned and disconnected. I feel like a freak.

When I envision happiness and a state of peace, I see myself being creative, being part of a larger whole, and being an individual but also a contributor. But what this is, I don't know.

8/22/98
It was a long difficult day. I wanted to overdose on laxatives and was really scared. I know that they could kill me or leave me unconscious. I didn't want to do that to Mom.
I feel so fat. I've lost complete control. I want to die.

8/23/98
In the middle of this crisis, I receive a letter from Rachel, breaking off our six-year friendship. I think she took the easy way out. It's so hard not to respond but I know I'll be a better person for it. I don't need to retaliate. It wouldn't change anything by having my say or making her feel bad. If anything, it would just reinforce her decision even more.
I don't think she's realized what she's done. I know that one day she will come to regret this. I know because I felt it myself with people I'm no longer in touch with.

Crisis Intervention: Mom, Allen, Cathy O., and Crisis Team Leader present
It was very difficult and painful. God was here because I was able to tell my truth. I broke down mid-way when I described how I came back from California because I started to feel suicidal. It surprised me when I broke down. We all did. I can't imagine how difficult that was for Mom and Allen to hear how I have been feeling.
It was hard to leave. This is so heart-breaking to everyone. But now I have no doubt about how I'm loved. I think I'll have the strength to get better.

Admitted to psychiatric unit for depression and safety:
8/26/98
The eating disorder isn't the problem. It's the sexual abuse. I can eat myself back to health but still feel like crap. That has been the case. I get well for a little while and then drop back down. And if it's not an eating disorder, it will be something else.
When I talked to Kathy on the phone she asked me, "are you ready for this?" I didn't know what she meant, but I said, "I

have to be." I guess she knows the road I'm embarking on; a road that she has avoided.

8/27/98

This place isn't really for me. There are people here who have mental illness, hear voices, and talk to them. During the night there were screamers. I dozed in and out of sleep. I may be sick, but I'm not one of these people. I don't know how I will get anything out of the meetings.

I haven't had an appetite. They don't monitor meals. I threw away my dinner and ate a few bran flakes at breakfast. Stepping on the scale, my weight hovered at 100 pounds.

I've completely gone into starvation mode. I've even stashed a couple of cookies, crackers, peanut butter & jelly in my drawer. I don't really intend to eat it. I just feel better for having it there.

Recovery entails scary factors. I should expect to gain 10-15 pounds. It means going out into the world, taking risks in relationships, and forming new ones. It means conquering fears in social situations, and ultimately, facing my fears with intimacy. Lauren, my case-worker, suggested more than anything that the eating disorder did act as a buffer to a romantic relationship. There's just no possible way to be close to someone and be keeping this secret. But she felt that when I'm ready, I would be able to do these things. She'd like to see me working on both issues, as they are intertwined.

8/28/98

My goal today is to increase my consciousness. Being aware of everything around me and of my senses and movements. I tend to wander off in my head, so I want to work on being in the present.

For breakfast I ate half of a bagel (80 calories) and half of a yogurt (60 calories) for a total of 140 calories. I stashed some dry cereal in my drawer.

I had difficulty sleeping. I woke up around 2:45 am and couldn't go back to sleep. I was given Tylenol and that helped.

Outcome of Family Meeting:
    I'll be staying here for another week. They want to make sure my medication is working and that I keep taking it. The other concern is that I don't have another program to enter right away. If I go home before the weekend, the chances of experiencing the same difficulties are high.

8/29/98
    Today was really rough. I woke up with a pounding headache and a slight stomachache. I could hardly walk straight. My blood pressure was 82/60.
    When I got to breakfast I couldn't eat. I took a bite of bagel and it hurt to chew. So I put my head on the table but I got reprimanded for that. I decided to choose oatmeal and yogurt instead since it didn't require chewing. I skimmed the top layer of oatmeal and slurped the 4- ounce yogurt. It helped reduce the pounding. I saw the connection between food and pain relief. I hadn't wanted to eat because I felt so horrible but it was eating that helped me feel better. My body needed food.
    I ate a little soup for lunch and dinner, a half piece of bread, a little scoop of egg salad, a few mini bites of veggie burger. I'm starting to feel out of control. Staff is on to me now with eating. I can't go anywhere after meals; not that I have a lot to purge.
    I got in trouble yesterday for the stashed food in my drawer. At first everyone thought I was bingeing because I had been taking food. But I was just saving it for when I could eat it. It wasn't going to happen. I felt really depressed after I had to throw out the food. I didn't like how the staff had handled the situation.
    Yesterday I had asked about having a different snack at night because I can't eat the sandwiches and chips that are served. However, I didn't know that you had to ask by 6:00 p.m. The Kitchen closes. I just assumed the food comes up when snack time arrives.
    It took me so long to decide whether to have an apple or not. I decided I would. When I asked the nurse, she had such an attitude about it. I hated myself for asking for an apple, for wanting an apple.
    I slid into depression. I didn't go outside. I didn't go to the

last meeting. I didn't go out for snack. I lay in bed in a trance. I felt alone. I couldn't process my feelings with the staff. I didn't feel like writing. I was angry. I thought of suicide but mostly as a fantasy, wondering how else I could do it without any pills or objects to hurt myself with.

I could crack my head against the wall. Suffocate myself with a pillow. Break the mirror for shards of glass. Drink shampoo. Hang myself from the showerhead.

These are really violent ideas. I've never thought so gruesomely. I wouldn't act out. They're just thoughts.

I went into the bathroom and sat in the dark. There I was able to let out real sobs. When I stopped crying, I listened to the tapping of my foot on the tile floor. It had a rhythmic beat that soothed me. But I felt like I was going crazy.

I had the idea of throwing up my medicine but I didn't do that. Instead, I tucked the pills under my tongue. I'm surprised they don't check. I spit them out.

8/30/98

I felt like I beat the system when I slipped away to my room unnoticed. I threw up breakfast in two heaves. I realized I hadn't eaten much but I felt triumphant anyway.

8/31/98

Daddy came! It was a great day. I was allowed four hours on pass. We went out for lunch (soup for me, chicken sandwich for him), then we browsed through the nearby mall where we both got books. After the mall, we sat in a little park across the street from the hospital, where Kathy would come to meet us. We talked pretty frank about the illness and abuse. Dad said that somehow I needed to make a pact with the devil, or God, or whatever so that I can see myself through this. It will take super willpower to beat this. Everyone seems to be aware that this is going to be a tough battle for me. I have to get better or I will die.

9/3/98

Plans for after-care are slow and frustrating. Insurance is an issue. Westwood doesn't accept MA Health. There are no free care facilities. Mass General no longer has an in-patient program. Although they do have an intensive outpatient program, they wouldn't even consider me unless I went in-patient. Their opinion was that I would die if I didn't gain weight soon. What is a sick girl to do who is becoming weaker by the minute? I barely have any strength. Every hopeless phone call drains me. No one in *this* hospital seems to take me seriously. There are no places outside the Boston area. Another option, maybe, is to consider NY State.

There's a way through God. Please let there be a miracle.

9/4/98

My goal is to be well for Christmas. I want to start believing that God will relieve me of this. He can take this from me. But I have to ask him to. I have to fully believe that Jesus died for me. He is ready to help. He will heal me. But I have to believe. I can't believe in my way anymore. It will kill me.

9/5/98

Back at home. I spent a lot of time in the shower just letting the hot water flow over me and caress my skin.

Mom, Allen and I are meeting with the lawyers this coming week to discuss my bills. I'll be filing for bankruptcy. A part of me feels bad because I wasn't responsible but I also feel hugely relieved that I don't have to worry about my debt anymore. There's a price to pay, but at least it will help me to get on with my life and I can put this behind me.

On disappointing family members:
9/9/98

That was the beginning of my depression. I became anxious. I don't know what provoked me. I have been talking about cutting my hair short and Peggy (my step-mom) was going to do it when I came up to visit in a couple of weeks. It was like watching a movie of myself. I got the scissors and went into the bathroom. I only intended to cut to shoulder length but I kept cutting. It gave me a calming feeling. And through the different lengths I recognized myself at different ages. It was weird.

I stopped only because I got a phone call. Otherwise, I probably would have kept going. Everything came crashing down.

Counting Bones

I scared the living daylight out of everyone. I couldn't explain my bizarre behavior. All I could think was that I couldn't cut myself but I could cut my hair. It seemed like a logical alternative.

Of course now I do look like a child. I look even tinier without the mask of hair. I think that's what scared Mom the most. She told me I was just skin and bones, a walking anatomy. We were both bawling and hugging each other. I have to take her word. There's no body inside my clothes. I'm all limbs with bones sticking out. I have no shape. It's just skin hanging off of bone.

I thought it was just family being over protective. Of course they would think I looked emaciated but I wasn't hearing it from anyone else. But that doesn't mean people don't see it. They just don't know what to say. And they don't want to hurt your feelings.

I don't see it. I look thin but not bony. I'm not 80 pounds. Everyone thinks I'm digging a grave but there are people far skinnier than I am who are still living. I weigh 98 pounds. With my short hair, sometimes I catch a glimpse of myself, and I think I look like a cancer patient. So on occasion I do see that I'm too thin. But I don't see emaciation like everyone else. I can still stand, walk, and carry on daily tasks. I'm not bed-ridden. I don't understand.

9/17/98

I feel a little shamed to think of this as some great accomplishment. Yeah, I'm thin, but everything in my life has been reduced to microscopic proportions. A ritual of holding my breath, scared, every morning that I've gained weight. It's odd that I feel that fear when that's not the case. Not only have I *not* gained weight but I've been steadily losing.

I want to be winsome, sophisticated and casual like the classic Audrey Hepburn. But something tells me that not even she was as thin as I am now. It's so confusing to put into context.

The things that linger inside me, the soft whisperings of my inner spirit, give me clues as to what would make me happy. Even if I can't attain them just now, goals are important to have. I want peaceful and serene settings as opposed to frenetic, pressure-cooker deadline jobs. My dream is to be an at home writer tapping away stories on my computer.

I think I have nothing to tell except for my eating disorder and post trauma. But there *is* more. I've got to have the courage to unveil myself *to* myself. There are lots of stories to tell but first, I have to live in its glory. I have to participate in this wonderful thing called life. I have to see the more complex dimensions of which I am rather than attempting to be shallow, hollow, translucent, and one-dimensional. It's a lie. You're not just one thing and it's okay to have many shades. It's okay to have dark shadows. But you also have the vibrant colors too. Nothing is good or bad. It's how you choose to feel and to be.

You have a duty to be here. You can't just check out because you're scared and uncertain. There are some things you just can't decide for yourself. You can't decide when to leave this earth. How do you know what God has planned for you? How do you know what your purpose is? If you're gone, you're gone forever. There's no other person like you. The universe greatly suffers. The people you were meant to encounter would mourn your loss too, although maybe not being aware of its origin. And for the people you love, it's just absolute selfishness and greed. You're only concerned with your own pain. You don't give regard to how crippling this would be. This would be a hollow grief that would never completely heal. Their lives would never be the same again.

It is for that reason that I've been able to hang on. But I realize that my continuing starvation is still a dance of deception. If I were to write a book, I'd title it "Counting my Bones" because it's such a stark contrast from "counting my blessings". The word bone is so eerie and spooky compared to the word blessing, which emanates light and warmth. Plus, counting my bones is real. There isn't a day or evening that goes by that I don't complete the ritual of retracing all my bones. There is mourning when I see these bones start to disappear behind the growth of flesh.

There is only one other certainty in my life. Writing has been consistent for me for over 10 years. Not once, have I ever doubted my ability to write. I feel confident about my capability. This embodies my spirit. I feel the most peaceful and serene when I am writing. Without my pen and paper, I'd be lost.

Writing requires me to be present and in the moment. I have to be conscious. I have to fill the well so-to-speak.

Counting Bones

9/23/98

    I dropped another pound to 96. I guess I'm burning more calories with all the housework.

Darren & Kerrie's wedding:
9/27/98

    I felt a little sorry for myself seeing all the couple's there. Does anyone know what it feels like to feel sick when the opposite sex touches you? I want to be married some day but right now I can barely get past introductions.

    My high school friend Jen was there. She immediately told me I was too thin and that she had been anorexic for many years. This is what she told me: basically, you have to feel your feelings. You can't avoid them. You have to face what's making you feel so bad. Be happy and love yourself. You're the most important person. If you don't love yourself then no one else can love you. Life is too short to be sad.

    It all seemed too easy. I wanted to ask her more questions but there's really no mystery. You just have to do the work. You have to move through it. And don't try to take short cuts and detours.

    The truth is I haven't gotten past the abuse. I have to deal with it. It makes me incredibly sad. But that was then and this is now. You can't change what happened but you can create your future. You can choose to be sad or happy. You can feel self-pity or self-love. It's really not as hard as you think it is. It's just going to take a lot of patience and commitment to change my way of thinking.

    I feel so afraid. I'm afraid of gaining weight. I'm slightly embarrassed by my thinness. Sometimes I am aware that I'm all limbs. Out on the dance floor, I knew I looked like a dancing skeleton, all arms and legs. And yet, I don't want my body to expand. I don't want to have curves. I'm afraid of my sexuality. I'm ice-cold frigid. I'm afraid of what lies beneath.

    Gaining curves means coming back into my body; feeling all its senses. When you starve yourself, it shuts down all your emotions. Eating really means coming alive again. You've been in a coma-like state for a long time. To have courage means feeling the fear but doing it anyway.

10/5/98
Weight is back up to 98 pounds and feeling fat. Have to "diet" again. I've felt full most of the time and I want to feel that gnawing hunger again. The only reason I know I'm hungry, in the literal sense, is that my stomach growls when I feel full. So even though I feel full, I still haven't eaten enough.

Alone for the weekend:
10/12/98
Bulimia came back in a vengeance. I would try to have a good day. It was going back and forth from kitchen to bathroom. All day Saturday and all day Sunday. I was able to break free to see a movie at least, but then I felt guilty. I didn't count the number of times I threw up. It had to have been at least 10x each day.

I was bored silly. I was sick of myself, being with me, having me as my own companion. Why couldn't I treat myself nicely this weekend? It was a perfect time to pamper myself and just relax but I had to beat myself up.

I haven't been writing. Now I'm just glad it's over. I had a choice whether to have a good weekend or not. I chose not. I almost said, "bad choice", but I caught it. No choice is good or bad. What I learn from any experience is **always** positive!

10/19/98
I've been living out of mind for several weeks. My interest in food is returning after weeks of indifference. I'm trying to get back in check. I look at pictures of skinny people in the media and I don't relate to them. I still feel pangs of envy, thinking, "God, I wish I could look like that" and it's a weird thing because, incidentally, I *do* look like that but it doesn't register with me.

On family support:
10/20/98
It's kind of a relief because it seems to take away the pressure. You won't get well over night. No one expects that of you. So I can just relax and do my best. There is no race and it's

better that I go about this slowly and cautiously so that I allow things to mend and heal. Just like when you have an injury, if you don't take care of it properly or push too soon or too fast, you're just going to set yourself back more. Or you'll make the condition worse.

I need to have a game plan. I need to have goals, short and long-term. If I don't have something to strive for then what is going to keep me motivated? If I don't have something to care about, then what's the point? Right now I'm floundering aimlessly. I think using the time to create goals is a good start. Everything is positive. Remember that there is perfection in everything. Rather than feel bad or useless, let's focus on what's positive about this free time. Feel good about it. Each day is a new day, so don't think about the string of days in succession.

Author's Note:
This next entry was recorded during the media's fury and obsession (which raged on for months) over the appearance of the then star of *Ally McBeal* after she showed up at the 1998 Emmy Awards in a dress that revealed she was unquestionably too thin. Although the actress denied rumors of being anorexic, it had a huge impact on me. For the first time, I had a visual image to measure myself by and could see why everyone was so upset. The fact that the whole world was alarmed about Calista Flockhart's weight sent a very strong message to me.

Is she or isn't she? The Calista Flockhart debate:
I'm thinking that if she's already lonely, having the whole world talking about you has got to be so hard. It's so hard just dealing with yourself let alone what millions of people are thinking. I can't imagine going to bed at night with that kind of burden, and then again in the morning, wondering how I'll face the day. It's got to be a nightmare for her.

My reflection on being in a support group:
10/26/98
The most striking thing is how I'm different in a group setting. I probably said more tonight than I ever did in all my time in the hospital. I feel much more open. It seems funny to feel

impatient because there's so much to say. I remember how stifled and terrified I used to be with being in a group setting. It was impossible to speak.

10/27/98
I got home close to 5 o'clock and had no idea what to plan for supper. There was nothing pulled out. I knew I wanted to use ricotta cheese but there was nothing to go with it. To use up different veggies in the refrigerator, I opted to make omelets, oil-free potato skins, Caesar salad and butternut squash soup. It was a spur of the moment decision. I was so proud of myself! Mom and Allen loved it too. I was so afraid of disappointing them with no dinner planned. Mom was especially exhausted. She deserved to have a freshly cooked meal. And eggs for dinner are a nice change of pace. I only want my consumption to be 300 calories, as I am trying to lose five pounds.

The only reason I guess I may be too skinny is that I fit into children's clothes. The only problem is that the sleeves and hemlines are too short. Naturally, they're not supposed to fit a 5'6" adult woman. Even the tag said the height requirement is between 4'10" and 5'0" and weight range of 84-96 pounds. I did notice a few people look at me strangely.

10/29/98
Can someone tell if you have low self-esteem by just looking at you? I don't have the telltale signs of stilted posture and downcast eyes. Sometimes I feel ashamed just walking down the street. I think people know and judge me just by looking at me. It's either a look of pity or a condescending smirk.

11/4/98
Feeling like my eating disorder is a moral issue. That everyone expects me to take control and know what to do. But I'm not in control and it's so painful to be in the meantime. I hate having this and I've hated myself for having this. But I mistake the disease for being part of who I am. If I can step outside of myself and see that the disease is separate from me and is killing me, it will give me the strength and stamina to attack it. This disease lies. It does not comfort you, provide relief, it is not a friend, and it

is not something you can have "once in a while". It will kill you. It has robbed you already of so many treasures. There is no time to mourn. There can only be joy in knowing that you've survived. Rejoice in who you are and what you've become.

People don't understand and if you're constantly struggling with that, it only keeps you stuck where you are. Stop worrying about what other people think and live your life for *you*. By God, don't you think it's time? You deserve to shine.

11/11/98
Within the last two days I've had two emotional breakdowns. It's not just crying, it's a paralyzing type of sobbing I've never experienced before, where I always end up crumpled on the floor. The other night I was trying to take my medicine, and as I was reaching for a glass in the cupboard, my hand just remained frozen there for a few minutes. I couldn't take the glass. I was crying so hard. I crumbled to the floor

I notice that I become very agitated by noise and a lot of things going on at once. The TV going, people walking around, three different conversations going on at once, people dropping things by accident...I hear a ringing sound in my right ear and I wonder if other people ever get that buzzing sound.

I'm alarmed when tears threaten to pursue, so I jump up to clean all the dishes. I don't know what's wrong with me. I retreat to my room and the tears come. What triggered this? I feel so bad because Kathy is here and I don't want to spoil her visit.

After she leaves, Mom comes in and asks me what's wrong. She's not aware that I've already been crying. Since I can't really answer, I'm just more confused, and she walks away seemingly upset about my lack of response. I don't want people to be mad at me for not being able to decipher my feelings. I shouldn't be feeling this badly. I don't deserve to feel this bad. I wonder when I'll ever feel good.

11/14/98
I'm starting a new medication, zyplexa, an <u>anti-psychotic</u>. The doctor told me not worry about the term. I'm not really psychotic. It works as an antidepressant and will help me feel more connected within myself. It will help me to be more in

control. It will also help me to gain weight because it stimulates appetite.

11/15/98
The missing piece of the puzzle, a part of my brain, can be realigned and then maybe I can feel normal. I have felt crazy trying to explain myself to a perplexed family. "Just try to be happy" or "You have to pull yourself together" are the typical responses. But how can I pull my *self* together if it is pretty much non-existent? This is what the medicine will do for me-the return of myself.

11/20/98
At around 11 o'clock this morning, Granddad died. I didn't know until I got home. Mom didn't want us to be upset all day and leave our jobs. I was meaning to visit Granddad this week. I can't make myself feel guilty. Maybe God wanted it that way. Uncle Johnny was there when he passed away so it helps to know that he wasn't alone. And he was sleeping so it was very quiet and peaceful. Still, it was such a shock when Mom spoke the words. My hands flew to my face. I was surprised by how quick my reaction was. I mean, I don't know what I expected. I loved him so much and I hope he knew that. He knows now. What makes me feel better, too, is that he's with Nana. They're united once more in heaven.

Thanksgiving Day:
11/26/98
It was more difficult than I imagined. I've felt really uncomfortable and anxious and yet I know the bloated feeling gives me a false sense of weight gain. It feels like I'm blowing up like a balloon.

It's been an emotional week with the passing of Granddad. In the midst of it, there's a lot of food around. This is really difficult. It's tempting to revert back but I know that I have to keep eating. It's never going to be easy. There's no easy way of getting through it. But it *does* get easier. I just have to get over this hurdle.

Fighting Strategy:
11/29/98

It's that "act as if" thing. Act out what you want in order to become it. You can't wait for recovery to happen. You can't wait for someone to tell you what to eat or what to weigh. Take that into your own hands. And you can feel better because you did it for yourself. Do not feel shame for heeding your own direction. Feel proud, because you do have the answers to your own questions.

11/30/98

I ate today even though I felt no real hunger pangs. For the first time, I feel determined to eat and to keep eating. I don't know what triggered it. Maybe Granddad had something to do with it. Remembering his life changes how I feel about my own. Times like these bring a family closer together, and in the togetherness, I've been able to eat.

12/1/98

I don't feel acute hunger. I never once felt hungry over the holiday yet I ate anyway. I never would have eaten that amount of food had I been alone. Perhaps I was able to cope by recognizing the communion and sacredness of sharing with family. However, now that moment has passed and I have to find another way to keep my resolve.

How I feel changes from day to day. I have to decide how I want to feel and how I want to be otherwise, I won't be prepared when I waver. I will falter- that is to be expected. Yesterday I felt good about my weight, today I don't. I confuse other people and myself with my contradictions.

I only took the medications for a few days. I abandoned it to try and control my weight a little longer. I gained weight on my own and now I wonder why I took the medication at all. I don't want a pill controlling my weight.

My resistance to the medication makes me question my commitment to health. I want to keep my size 0 frame. Sometimes, I think I am so ready to let go that building up my size would actually be appealing. But then I look at the clothes that used to be loose, and now fit, and I don't feel good anymore.

The greatest irony is that, by societal standards, I have the body type that people envy. When I'm maintaining a good weight, I'm not a person who gains that easily. Even when I do, I lose it just as quick. I am one of those people who can eat pretty much what she wants. However, that doesn't mean what I want is a cheeseburger and fries. But considering how much of a sweet tooth I have, then I guess I would have a fast metabolism.

I think my anxiety was triggered when I saw my former childhood friend, Karen, last night. Back in high school I always felt frumpy and fat next to her petite bikini-clad body. She was thin when she got married three years ago. Now she must be 30-40 pounds heavier. I don't know if quitting smoking did it or having a baby. I hate to cast judgement. She probably doesn't care. I would just never want that for myself. I think I do have a secret fear that I'm going to get fat like that. It's a fear not based in reality.

Realistically, based upon weight history, I'd most likely bounce back to pre-pregnancy shape after having a baby. During pregnancy I probably wouldn't carry a lot of extra weight. I shouldn't even be worrying about events that are way into the future, but they are still roadblocks.

Now that I think about it, I don't think it's a coincidence for me to think about pregnancy. I have an intense hatred for my period and I'm basically frigid. Aren't they all related? This is all about sexuality.

12/3/98

Last night was extremely difficult where I felt like hurting myself again. It was already a weepy day when Mom decided to yell at me for no good reason. She still insists on talking to me from another room where I cannot hear her, and then gets mad at me when I don't respond right away. She says I'm in my own"fantasy" world, and if she didn't nudge me, then I'd never take care of my own affairs. She doesn't seem to understand that her constant nagging just makes things worse. Her, Allen, and Kevin, all they're nit-picking don't give me any ammunition. It just makes me confused and angry. I don't channel my anger into something positive. Again, I am thinking of dying. I just want to be left alone. I just want to go to sleep and not wake up for a while.

Everyone says how selfish it is to end your own life. They even put religion into it to add more guilt. But I don't feel like I'm living for me or hanging on for me. And this whole process of trying to get well doesn't feel like my own journey. Everyone is telling me what to do, how to feel, and what to think.

A plan of deterrence:

Thinking of Cailin always brings a smile to my face. Don't you want to see her grow up?

12/5/98

I feel so angry. I hate my body. Sometimes I just want to cut myself when faced with my image in the mirror. I can tell that I haven't lost any of the excess weight (from Thanksgiving week) even though I haven't been eating much. I could kick myself for gaining it, being so careless.

I understand I am being very cruel and hateful towards myself. The reality is I am intensely lonely. My anger comes from not feeling heard and frightened that I won't be. I can't stand being encased in this body.

12/6/98

Turning my anger towards the right source is the key. I cannot battle the state, or the system alone. I will have to play the game to get what I need. It is too draining. I have to get people to advocate for me. They may not understand me but they understand the tricks of the trade.

My reasoning is simple. I will die if I don't get the care I need. This is absolute bottom for me. This is the worst bout I've ever been through. And it won't get better without specific intensive treatment.

This is a major wound and all I'm getting right now are Band-Aids. The gap of the wound just gets bigger and bigger- I will bleed to death if I can't stitch it up. If you're in an accident, a hospital has to take you regardless of insurance. It should be the same procedure here. So they're going to turn me away because of money? I wonder how many people die because of this.

I'm not suggesting that I'll be cured, but even the

medication would be more effective if I were hospitalized. I'm sure that it can't work as well if I'm not eating properly. If I'm nourished, and receiving support around that, it will help me to be more focused-and stronger-to deal with my issues. I have to deal with this inside out. Dealing with outside issues without support for the eating disorder only makes it worse.

As to why hospitalization didn't work before? Lack of prevention and knowledge. I know more now than I did then. When you know more, you can apply more.

It's hard enough to fight this illness myself. I can't fight the system. It makes me feel worse. I feel like I'm dying inside.

12/7/98
I know other people in the family will think that I shouldn't be taking this route. If I were so sick then how would I have the energy to commute (for outpatient care)? It gives me energy knowing that I'm getting real help. I can't waste precious energy worrying about what others think.

12/9/98
I feel sort of like a fraud because I can't really be an anorexic. I'm out of medical danger. I weigh more. I mentioned this in therapy. I don't feel worthy of the diagnosis. Yet, it's more than weight. Weight is a very small matter. Eating is not a large focus either, although it is a strong component. When I start feeling deserving and worthy in other areas of my life, it will naturally spill over into my eating habits.

Also talked about breaking down my long-term goals into shorter increments so that I can see progress building. I want food to be my friend, and not something to dread or fear. I want to enjoy eating and be proud of it. I thought of my college floor mate, MJ, today for that reason. She was always so gusto about eating, making yummy yelps of delight. In a way, it almost seemed like an orgasmic experience. I don't know of anyone else who expressed that much enthusiasm about food. Most people just murmur politely, "oh, this is good". MJ was unique in that way and I admired her for it. And, for the record, she was thin.

12/12/98
    Today I felt "good". I felt happy! I'm glad I decided to go with Mom to help her with her shopping. I think what made me happy is that I really was a big help to her. Everything she got was something I picked out. She had a very hard time finding a dress for Kathy's wedding but I wouldn't let her settle for desperation. Finally, we found a dress that was simple, graceful, and elegant. You have to feel good about what you wear. If I hadn't gone with her, she would have come home cranky and dispirited. She still came home exhausted but at least she had peace of mind.

12/13/98
    I'm starting to adjust to weighing more; considering, perhaps, that I *won't* lose anymore. I don't feel as upset. Now I'm moving into a comfortable zone. However, I don't know about weighing more.
    My words alone cannot belie my truth, but I'm determined to get well. I just want to eat and be happy. I think I'm growing weary of being this small. I'm finding it to be increasingly uncomfortable. I think I just had to live it out and decide that I don't want to live like this.

On being told my opinion doesn't count:
12/17/98
    I felt absolutely sick to my stomach. It reminds me of something. Shut up. Just shut up. Nothing I say matters. I'm just invisible; seen but not heard.

12/28/98
    Scribbling down ideas and goals for New Year. 1998 was so god-awful. It was a really tough year, for a lot of people, on all levels; publicly, nationally, and individually. Here's hoping that '99 will be much happier and peaceful.
    It's got to be a good year for the end of the century! We have to go out with a bang! I already can't wait for next year. I'm sorry that Christmas is over. Next year will be more prosperous.
    I want to like myself and be happy with who I am. I want to feel worthwhile and loved. I want to be this for myself. I have to

reach inward to bring this up. I have to reflect and be quiet. Listen. Pay attention to small details. Look to nature. The smallest moments bring the greatest pleasures.

I haven't liked myself this year or things I've done. I want to quietly acknowledge these things to myself and with God and activate change. I've been careless, thoughtless, and removed. Forgive yourself. You were acting out.

I want to start moving towards my future, to open my heart, to allow events to happen. I want to marry and have two kids. A boy and a girl would be nice. I don't need to play the field to find who makes me happy. I've never dated and I don't see myself dating. I know that whoever my husband is will be my friend and my first and only. This decision is not based upon religious beliefs, and it may be subject to change, but for now it is a declaration of love to myself. It has to be a completely safe and trusting atmosphere. At least in marriage, you can absolutely be certain how the person feels about you, and there isn't "the morning after" effect.

My husband will also have a great family that is loving and supportive. His parents will not be divorced. Having another set of parents and sister and brother in-laws to fulfill what I didn't have as a child is important to me. The chain of disconnection will be broken with me. Indeed, this is what I want, and so, let's stay focused on where I want to go and who I want to be. Anorexia doesn't fit into the picture.

12/29/98

I'm feeling restless. Spent most of the day helping Mom search for misplaced items. She keeps muttering to herself, "I don't understand". You get what you put out. Thus, she keeps having the same routine repeated again and again. I have little to complain about though. I just wish she could enjoy herself more. Eventually she did go out and she's going out with "the girls" tomorrow.

I want to start feeling good about myself. I still feel so dead conscious. Walking around tuned out most of the time. I want to take small steps to getting back in touch with myself. I want to treat myself holy, the spiritual being that I am, and also to celebrate and acknowledge that in others.

I feel so fat. I'm filling out in places that used to be concave. My ribs don't stick out as much and my stomach is bigger. I hate to keep obsessing about my weight.

New Year's Day
1/1/99

It is so weird to write '99! But I welcome it. As I write, I am feeling happy and content. It feels great to be in a New Year. It just feels like a chance to renew and start fresh. I'm feeling so much better. Of course still experiencing discomfort with eating but I'm trying to stay focused.

Ask God for help. I want to be close with God again. I want to really build my faith in him again. '98 was an absolute wreck and chaos. It was a direct reflection of my thoughts. I didn't believe and as a result my world caved in.

1/3/99

I feel inadequate for not having money, for not being in a job, to still be living at home. However, I'm trying not to dwell on these thoughts. Remember that what you think comes back to you. Change your thoughts to what you want to create in your life. These things will come in time. You have to think about what you want. Prioritize. When I work, I definitely have to save my money.

If you were not present in a room and your name came up, or someone was to describe you to someone else, what would you like to hear them say about you?

I still admire people who are outgoing, fun, and sparkly. Sometimes I just feel so dull and unattractive in looks and personality. I suppose it's normal for everyone to feel that way sometimes. Everyday I want to feel as positive as possible. I want to feel as happy as I can be.

Every morning is a new morning. Every day the sun rises. You may not see it behind clouds or rain but you can believe it's there. You can find prediction in an unpredictable world. You can find comfort in things you can count on such as the sun rising. Most importantly, you can believe in God's love. He never stops loving you. I don't want to hurt myself. I don't want to do things that make me feel bad about myself. I'm afraid of someone reading this, but if I can't admit this to myself, then how can I begin to reconcile? I only want keep this between God and me. And perhaps I should bring it up in therapy. I don't know.

I've just always prided myself on being trustworthy and honest. I can't tell a lie but not telling a lie is a lie in itself. I've shoplifted. At first it was "little things" like a tube of makeup and candy. I stole food from supermarkets. Then I took magazines. But I could see a pattern building, the same way any other compulsion builds momentum. First, you believe that you'd never do something like that. Then you get away with something "little". But little gets a little bigger. Or you say you won't do it again. But when you know you cannot pay for something, it's hard to ignore the lure. It came to a hilt in the last couple of weeks. I said to myself that I would never steal clothing. First, because I was really afraid of store security. Second, because then it would *really* deem me a thief. Fortunately, I haven't been caught, but I don't want to do it anymore. I'd die if my family knew. I feel uncomfortable when Kevin talks about theft in his store.

Why did I do it? I don't know if it's a coincidence, but my purging has diminished. It was another kick, a behavior of control, or to prove how bad I was. Is it possible just to let it go without telling anyone? I can make myself stop before it becomes a real problem. I've broken a majority of the Ten Commandments.

I can't have faith unless I'm honest. When does inquisitiveness and curiosity border on gossip? I hate wanting to know. I'll be the person asking, "What? Who?" if I've missed part of a conversation. However, I think its part of having been the youngest child. I felt left out a lot of times.

I think the biggest thing is forgiveness. Forgive yourself. Know that God has forgiven you. And forgive other people their moments of weakness because you've certainly had your own. Be compassionate, open, and understanding. Even when people disappoint you or make you mad. It is most important then. Seek to understand. Do not close your mind or your heart. Other people can choose to be narrow, bigoted, and insensitive. They are the ones who need compassion. Think of how hard it must be to live like that. I believe everyone is good at heart. Some are just afraid to show it, or they have a longer journey.

It will come that you will see God in your life again. You'll feel his warmth, love, and light. The truth is, he's never left you.

It's just that to accept him is to accept yourself. Acceptance actually hurts. Why does it hurt so much to let go of pain? Why is it so hard to love yourself? Because to get there really hurts. You have to face those feelings.

When I think about not eating, I need to remember where I want to go. There is no gain from being too skinny. You can't be whom you want to be if you allow your life to be over-ruled with this obsession. God, every day I have to fight. My butt and thighs are bigger. Big fucking deal, right? There are worst things in life. It's not about your size. It's about control. When you feel like you can't control your body, you're powerless. Sometimes, no, just about always I feel so overwhelmed with the world, never mind my space. It feels big and scary. When I go outside, it's akin to looking under the bed for the boogey man, or checking the closet for monsters. When I was little, I was deathly afraid of the basement. The coal stove was down there. The pipes in the wall extending from the stove looked dark and menacing. Anything could jump out.

Why couldn't I be an actress? I feel so sad about that.

1/11/99
I am incredibly blessed for having completed the trilogy of *Conversations with* God. It is extraordinary. All the answers are in those books. When you're full of God's spirit, you'll never be hungry. Of course it is not complete. It continues on. The dialogue continues. The process will go on forever. I am so glad I know this NOW. I feel like I've been saved years of heartache.

1/12/99
I'm trying to fulfill something that will make me normal, stable, basically conforming to what is considered predictable and safe. Truth is, I do know myself, and I can't remain static for too long. I truly am a free spirit.

I am excited, overjoyed, and yet I dread this too, for what I really want in life is to still be an actress.

1/17/99
I was watching outside my window and noticed a squirrel scurrying up the branches of a tree. It was high up, and then it

jumped from tree to tree! It was so cool. When I was a little girl, I used to love watching squirrels. See, I connected with an innocent and happy time in my childhood. I also loved watching birds and looking for bird nests.

1/19/99
    I allowed myself four slices of toast with jam, not eaten in one sitting. The bread was low calorie so it equaled one serving of bread. 160 calories plus 50 or so for the jam. I felt really full. I'm afraid it's still going to turn into fat because my body thinks it's a feast.
    I really slid back this week. I'm obsessed with the mirror again. I'm feeling fat. I'm depressed about being here. I need to stay focused on building my independence. Don't give in to depression. Don't feel like you have to figure out everything by tomorrow. It's going to take time.
    It always is that when I decide on a plan, I'm really happy, excited, and HOPEFUL, but then the pressure begins. That is, what I put on myself. My fear is that I'm never going to amount to anything. I'll be a street hustler or doing something cheap and cheesy. I'm afraid of not having a family of my own.
    What you fear, you create. Wow. My biggest fear is being alone. I'll be broke and poor with no stability or direction. Wandering aimlessly with a vacant stare. I don't want to become that.
    This is a landmark. It's so great to know what you're afraid of, specifically, so that you can work on it.

1/20/99
    In therapy today, I talked about my premature birth and events surrounding that; how I had the intuition and sensitivity to know that I was needed. I couldn't die. My spirit was defined then. The dynamics started then. This paradoxical image of me as feisty/strong/independent versus fragile/weak/meek has interchanged throughout my whole life.
    I see myself as strong, fierce, and independent. This is how I want my life to be. My family, on the other hand, sees me as being fragile, meek, and vulnerable. They question my motives and give me unsolicited advice and lessons thinking that I don't

know better. They don't have insight into me. What they want to teach me is not what is important to me. I don't understand why they can't stop to ponder that maybe I have lessons for them by what is important to me.

This paradox keeps flipping. They keep changing their minds about what they want me to be. They hold me up as stoic then kick me down. No wonder why I second-guess myself. How I demonstrate my strength is that I don't listen, I have my opinions, I haven't had men problems, and I've traveled.

It's hard for me to be me when I'm dependent. Not just financially but emotionally too. I haven't quite figured out the latter yet. Mom and I have a unique and intense bond because of the way we started out. She had reason to be more protective than usual. The fear of losing me was quite real.

Mom doesn't realize this but she depends on me. She has an investment in keeping me dependent because it will keep me close. I see in Mom what I don't believe she knows about herself. I see her as a very strong woman but I think she sees herself as weak. Which is why everyone rallied around her during our estrangement. If Mom accepts my independence and strength, then she also has to recognize that within her. And gosh darn it that's fucking scary.

Jo-D (my therapist) believes that I have the most potential to go the furthest, at least, personality-wise. It could also be professionally speaking as well.

I talked about my blocks. Why can't I let myself be brilliant? Because people will look at me. I'll be recognized. The shame factor comes up. I don't deserve it crap. I want to eliminate this.

Therapy is like working on a puzzle or an equation. I have to fill in pieces and test different quotients. I'm planning stages up to where I want to be. This time, everything is thought through and I'm totally prepared. I want to be happy and at peace.

1/21/99

It was a constructive group tonight. I took a risk and confronted my feeling stifled inside the group. I felt frustrated with not feeling the space to jump in with what I have to say. Even before it gets said, it doesn't feel worthwhile anymore. I don't feel heard and I don't feel worthy. I don't want to feel the inclination to raise my hand. I don't know how to do it. I don't know how to draw attention to myself.

That's what it is. BINGO! As I'm thinking about how to say my words, the moment has passed, and I feel even more self-conscious. I think it's about, "am I worthy of being heard?" Being heard is a whole new ballgame. It's exciting and exhilarating that, yes, I matter and people want to know me, and it's so new and scary. Moreover, to speak up, to speak for myself, let alone any other cause, means that I own my space in the world. Indeed, I'm not comfortable there, but everyday I will fight for my space and my right to be here.

I think I am so protective of my own boundaries that I'm afraid of unwillingly invading that of another. More deeply, I'm afraid to trust myself, so I'm reluctant to trust others. I'll start trusting myself when I stop allowing people to speak for me or make me feel unheard. I will stop listening to the people who second-guess me and seek the ones who believe in my inner strength.

I will learn to trust my own voice, even if on some days, it is just a little whisper. It is the one constant that shall never leave me. Do not be afraid. It is your friend. It will guide you through the night.

It felt good to release my emotion to the group. Everyone was glad that I did. Despite having the struggle of not knowing where to fit in, I privately acknowledged that I was the one to bring anger into the group. I was willing to say I was mad to the other members. I may let things ride but the time always comes that I do stand up. For me, I just need to take those punches sooner.

I'm also a person who does not like to waste words. I choose my words thoughtfully. I do not like to talk. I like to communicate. People who talk a lot don't know how to listen. It is through listening that I have learned the most about myself. Thus, when I do talk, it is with meaning. There's a lot more depth to language than just words.

Why do we stop with words? Why do we get wrapped up in words? Shall we go beyond this limit? Can we find a whole new realm of communicating? What if we had one day of silence? Declare it a holiday when we all go inward to reflect. We seek other ways to express ourselves to loved ones. What would happen? We may just find valuable discoveries and solutions!

1/24/99
    Presently, I'm watching the Golden Globe Awards and I'm grinning ear to ear. It's so exciting. It's the night when motion pictures and television industries come together. It's great when there are surprising wins. There's big competition. When I watch, it ignites my passion to be a part of it all. It's a gift to be amongst such extraordinary work and artists.

1/26/99
    OK. I don't like how my life is. I don't like me. I've always prided myself on being honest and trustworthy and now I feel like I'm more curious bordering on nosy. My mind has eroded from tabloid publicity, and it's harder for me to keep things at bay. I'm not interested in keeping anyone's secret.
    I am more embarrassed about stealing than having the problem of an eating disorder. I have to confess. I have to come clean. I don't want any family knowing but I should bring it up in therapy and somehow find restitution with God. I don't believe in Catholic confession so how do I make a fresh start? What will I do?
    You know you can't continue on this way. It's just another way to feel bad about yourself. I don't want to get in trouble but you can't change something you won't admit to. It's not enough to make a deal with yourself. You have to tell another person.

1/27/99
    I did not mention the shoplifting to Jo-D. Maybe it's something I can forget about. This doesn't have to be a disease.
    I mentioned my role in the group last week. My difficulty ranges from having been violated. The piece that was taken away from me is the validity of my own voice. I feel like I need permission from others and from myself to speak. However, others aren't aware what I'm thinking. What would be helpful is using interjector statements to make people aware that I have something to say. My anger and frustration comes from being stuck with my thoughts and not expressing them in the moment

they occur. However, since I eventually get around to it, it indicates that I know what I have to say is valuable.

My feeling "stuck" is the anxiety I feel surrounding the steps I need/want to take. You have a range of choices, and if something doesn't work out, you can't blame it on anyone.

Mom agreed to go to a session but "not all the time". I understand. I'm not expecting her too.

I also feel stuck because I'm not being fulfilled. In the end, I'll be someone different from what they wanted me to be. The ultimate question is, SO WHAT? They can't argue against me being happy with what I choose to do in life.

In one year I would like to be in my own apartment, be acting in a play or troop, be in a writing class, a book club, and have some money in the bank. The more I'm out there, the more opportunities I have. Bottom line is I just want to BE happy. So...pursue those things that make you happy! You'll meet people along the way and develop a circle of friends. Enjoy music, art, coffeehouses, movies, books, dancing, and anything new! I believe that if I'm happy then the term "success" just happens naturally.

With each choice I make, I'm carving my way. This is my journey. I wish I didn't care about what people think. I'm creative and unique. I'm in touch with that part of me. If people react, it probably comes from a place of envy or coveting. You become unhappy when you don't follow your own lead. Appreciate your uniqueness. Be glad that you're in tune with your spiritual and creative side. Take pride in your values. I've been morally corrupt with stealing but I won't get involved with the wrong man, have children too soon, or lead a predictable lifestyle. As Jo-D encouraged me, "Go forth in the world and be the creative and unique person that you are".

1/29/99

I'm feeling great here in NY. Cailin is such a joy. She's fully walking. She recognizes me. I feel like we have a relationship now. It feels so wonderful.

I've seen some pictures of myself at Kathy's wedding and over the holidays. I can see that my arms and legs still look skinny and that's *after* putting on eight pounds.

Counting Bones

Whenever I come to NY I always eat more. It's disconcerting.

1/31/99

Home. I'm glad to be away from NY even though I miss Cailin. She was so funny at her 1st birthday party. She lapped it up, dug right into her cake, and had a jolly time.

But I feel like the loser of the family now. They ask me about jobs and they don't get it. However, I'm reading this book that's helpful, "Something More: excavating your authentic self". I should and need to stop seeing myself through their eyes.

Pay attention to the small moments in which you dishonor yourself. It's the little and subtle ways that you damage yourself.

2/1/99

I feel tired. I threw up three or four times today so that I wouldn't digest any food. My weight is up to 106 from 104. I was still trying to lose at 104 pounds. I'm still consciously active in my disordered eating. I don't want to gain weight. I have no intention. If my weight creeps up to 105 or more, I eat a lot less and/or throw up more often. It's a conflict inside me. Even though I'm well above the critical low of 95 pounds, I don't feel much different.

The medication makes me feel less cloudy about things. I feel more in the here and now, but the eating disorder is still there. Its grip doesn't feel as painful as it was six months ago, but every single day my weight is an issue. It's in the back of my mind all day.

I have this surging compulsion that I've been toiling with to go on a weight loss spree. I haven't acted on it yet. Logically, I know I won't feel better, but emotionally, I ache to be there. The high of feeling nothing. Feeling light as air and to be floating on air. I just want to tumble once into the dark abyss. But what frightens me is that "just this once…" can prove to be the last. I just don't feel confident. I don't feel a complete conviction against anorexia. I'm not sure if I can give it up completely. I'm probably one of those borderline people who engage in this deadly dance throughout life.

For the most part, I don't really like to eat, at least not in the traditional sense. I hate myself when I eat against my own nature such as this past weekend. I find myself eating just because everyone else is and the schedule is different. I don't like to eat a lot at any one time. I always eat more when I go to NY. I half-kidded that I should visit more often.

I want to shut down my sense of taste. I just don't want to be burdened with it.

2/2/99

I killed my appetite today. I went grocery shopping and I tucked a Balance bar inside my purse. It was incredibly stupid. They nailed me, even for something that small. It was unbelievably stupid. I could have paid for it. I didn't, and there's a reason, but I don't know quite what it is. Otherwise, I wouldn't keep doing it! I can't go back to the store ever again. Hopefully, they won't call me back with a court order, because it is so over. I would rather kill myself than have anyone know about this because this *isn't* me. I'm not a thief. I don't get a kick out of this.

All I do know is that I resorted to this uncharacteristic criminal behavior because I needed to feel more ashamed and guilty; an extreme form of self-sabotage. I never wanted to be caught, but on some level, I was acting out from a place of feeling neglected and unheard.

I went straight to Cathy O's because she would be the only person I could talk to and feel safe with. It was really hard but I did it. And she understood. As a kid I was purely straight lace. I suppressed everything. I had no form of expression, no outlet to vent feelings I didn't even know I had. When other kids acted out or got rebellious, that was healthy for their time and age. Shoplifting is always wrong but it illustrates a point. All that suppression is erupting for me now, and it's coming out in self-destructive ways.

This is not about money. I had money. It's about the sexual abuse. I needed to feel like an ugly-rotten person. The pay-off is blocking out my fear; being afraid of this monster only the monster isn't the person who abused me. He is gone, so far back in the past, and living his own life now. Does he feel as rotten and ugly as I do? Does he want to die at the thought of being found out? Was I playing that out myself? He fucked with my brain and my body and what is left in its place? I think the anorexia is all about blasting that being into non-existence.

The one thing he can't take is my soul. I can starve my body down to nothing but I cannot escape my soul because my soul is the All of Me. This does not define my spirit. I wish I could minimize the abuse to just an event that happened. For something that is not supposed to define the All of Me, it sure feels like that's all there is.

2/3/99

I'm at the Coffee Bean for a few moments of reflection, after seeing Jo-D. I talked to her about the shoplifting, shared my writings about it, and also the compulsion to starve and lose weight.

She said I hit every element that she was thinking of. Although she hasn't done a lot of work with shoplifting, of the cases she's seen, a similar thread weaves out. Most people who have this compulsion were kids who were not emotionally given to. The stealing is like taking in and feeding yourself. She agreed with me on the factors of not feeling worthy, not feeling deserving, and feeling rotten and ugly.

I see myself through his eyes. What do I need to do to start seeing myself through my eyes? Get angry! Perhaps I shoplifted to get angry enough with myself. I can move towards forgiveness but I have to feel the anger first.

Jo-D thought it was interesting that this started happening six months ago, right around the time I started to deal with this again. I can make conscious choices now. When I feel the compulsion to take something or abuse myself, I can say to myself, "no, I'm not going to do that today. He's not going to win. I will not put a checkmark in his column". The more I practice, the less urgent the compulsion will be.

I do feel so much better for having talked about it. Jo-D thanked me for sharing my journal. That was a choice I didn't have to make. We're going to start slowly going into the sexual abuse but I have to be physically stable. I might not be ready or I might be okay.

As far as "borderline" people who do battle anorexia throughout life are usually able to pull out of it. During periods of high stress, you may resort to old unhealthy mechanisms but it usually peters out.

I haven't made a 100% commitment to beating anorexia. Jo-D can't help me there but I can develop more strength in that area. Part of the fear is that I'll gain weight and I'll still have this internal battle. She says that will go away. It will take time but it will go away. I can reach my full potential. I deserve to be my true authentic self. I deserve goodness, love, and adoration. My soul is beautiful and unique. I'm deserving and worthy of all good things.

2/10/99

I feel overwhelmed, sad, unhappy conflicted. I don't know where to start. How do I start to feel good? I was telling Jo-D today how impoverished I feel inside. If I could draw a picture of what I looked like inside, it would be a cold, barren desert with gray ashes and two sprigs of weeds. Everything else is dead. Nothing can grow. How do I begin to nurture it into a garden? It seems like a good simile. As winter wanes into spring, I hope my spirit will follow. I hope I can become alive again.

God, How do I become a friend with you? How do I feel close to you again? Please help me.

2/11/99

I felt a little better today. I slept until nine o'clock and then I took a one-hour nap at noon. I guess I was overtired.

I tried to relax. I lit my vanilla candle, a Christmas gift from Dad, for the first time. The flickering flame was soothing. I cleaned my room. I picked up the rest of the house and washed the floors. I made a Chinese dinner of shrimp and lo-mein. Today I did feel appreciated. Especially when Allen told me he has to have his knee reconstructed all over again. He said, "don't leave, don't move anywhere". That tells me they know I've been helping out.

I just chewed a million pieces of gum. I have to stop doing that. They have calories.

2/15/99

I read the book, "A child called It" in one sitting. The subject wasn't easy to read but it was easy to get through

Counting Bones

because the print was large and there were seven chapters in all. I gather that some people wouldn't be able to finish because the details are so grim. However, the eventual triumph of survival illuminates the story with hope and faith. This book is a miracle. I'm grateful to have read it. Whenever I feel down on myself, I can think about Dave Pelzer and what he endured. Both his parents betrayed him. The mother who tortured him and the father who stood by and did nothing. My parents might disappoint and hurt me but thank God for whom they are. This I must remember in moments of strife.

I feel depressed too. The darkness had an effect on me no doubt. I relate to the fear of not knowing what's going to happen next, looking to the other parent for comfort, terrified when she leaves.

I can't imagine being starved to death. His mother wouldn't feed him as punishment for not finishing his chores on time. He was weak, so he couldn't move fast enough, which meant he would not get food.

I wonder how the author feels about food today. If he had been a girl, she would have been a prime candidate for developing an eating disorder. It happens to men too, but not as much.

I feel fat. I think I look fat. I've been eating more. This is what I ate today:
Cereal bar, banana, pudding, cup of soup, five crackers, yogurt, slice of toast with a thin spread of peanut butter and jam.

I just had a flash of insight, sort of a forgotten truth. Whatever you dream in who you want your parents to be, you can find it in God. He's the Father and Mother of us all. What's great about God is that he allows you your freedom to decide who you want to be and become. He doesn't try to second-guess you or tell you what you *should* do. He lets you figure that out for yourself. You may learn the hard way but he doesn't hold judgement. He kind of gives you a gentle push, even when you've disappointed him. Then again, God is never disappointed. He feels disappointed for how you feel, but not in who you are.

The highest betrayal is the betrayal of self. It is taking me a very long time to stop betraying myself. It scares me to think about stopping. I'm living my life with one foot in and one foot out.

I've been stable for a good few months but I'm still trying to make up my mind which way to go. I can't stand the in between. I'm not really sick but I'm not really well either. Do I want to live like this? I'm scared to venture across the threshold. I'm scared of what's out there.

Lent began yesterday and although I don't feel like I'm a practicing Catholic, I can still honor Jesus on my own. I want to read the Bible. That's one step to bridging the gap between God and me. I know God is still here as always. It is me that is divided. I've forgotten my significance and magnificence! I can find it again.

2/23/99

I've experienced a different kind of misery these last couple of weeks. It's the misery of when you step from one ledge to another. In this case, stepping away from the grips of anorexia towards health. I've been eating regularly. I eat snack-size meals from 3-6 times a day.

I've waited so long to reach a good place. I'm not bubbling over but I feel okay. I feel stable. My emotions are in check. I'm clearer about things. I don't feel as ethereal or transparent. I feel more in control of me. I'm in control of *it* or at least I'm approaching that point. It feels very odd. I think of six months ago and I kind of yearn to be that wispy girl again.

Yesterday I struggled with taking my medicine. I understand the connection. I keep taking it because I don't want to return to despair and desperation. I don't want to be hospitalized. I've reached that point when it feels like everything is normal so I don't need medicine, but this is really only the beginning. This is also the time when the real process of recovery can begin. I've come away from crisis to stability. I can start to focus on some issues without the fear of falling back. I don't feel like I'm on shaky ground.

2/24/99

I ate a salad with feta cheese in it and real ranch dressing for lunch today. I've just made the observation that an outside observer couldn't assume that I'm anorexic because I eat. I still guzzle Diet Coke but you can see me eating. I don't know how I feel about that.

I'm uncomfortable every time I make the choice to eat. Eating just happened. All of a sudden recovery just happens. It's an invisible thing, like God, but it's still at work. Suddenly, it just made sense to eat something in the morning, afternoon, and evening. Things that were impossible before are now possible. Whereas before it was hard to eat, even to think about eating, now it's becoming harder *not* to eat. The more effort it takes, the more I realize that the turning point has come. This is the time you decide, "I'm not going back". I still want to be thinner but I can't.

2/25/99

Therapy was good. I read the last two entries. The battle is between deserving and undeserving. The wispy girl I yearn to be is someone who doesn't feel deserving. The young woman I am today *feels* more deserving but I'm struggling with it. I want to keep moving forward.

You can externalize the anorexia. It is not you it is an IT. I realize I'm not alone in this. Jo-D is helping me.

2/27/99

I slipped into a serious bout of depression tonight. I'm still struggling to keep taking my medicine. It's twisted that when I feel bad is the time I don't want to take it. If I don't take it, then I'm blowing six months of hard work. It's insane. Unless you really want to kill yourself, don't go there. I hate feeling despair.

I'm really mad with Kevin but there's nothing I can do about it but let go. I tried talking to him and he rebuffed me. He doesn't want to hear this. He thinks I talk way too much and should just keep doing. I tried to tell him that it takes a combination of both but he doesn't see it that way.

It's my own damn fault. I do things to make myself feel worse. Kevin is not the person to go to for empathy. I don't understand him anymore than he understands me. Why do I need his approval? Why does his opinion of me matter so much? He and Dad are just alike. They don't operate on an emotional level. We're complete opposites. It's no use trying to clarify yourself to them because they see your "talking" as part of the problem. You're just being self-indulgent and immature, as if age has anything to do with it.

Kevin is totally linear and scientific in his thinking. He's not spiritual and doesn't really believe in God. How do you expect him to respond to you?

2/28/99

I'm still feeling sad. Kathy and Peter were over for dinner and they called Kevin. So I talked to him too. Inadvertently, I apologized because I didn't have anything else to say. He refused to respond so it's no use trying to explain.
Later in the evening...

I'm feeling a little better. Occupation is a cure. I watched "Touched by an Angel" that I could relate to somewhat; feeling different and trapped within the family. I don't want to be bound by expectations. Let's say I decide to lead an artist's life, does that mean I'm wasting it? It's a matter of perception. There was a great line delivered by guest star, Bill Cosby, whose angelic character told the father, "what you hated in your son is God's gift to him". God inspired in the son to leave and go live the life of which he desired. God gave this to him because he knew he didn't have a lot of time. The son would die of cancer.

I don't know how to function in a family where no one wants to hear from you. Only surface superficial stuff is tolerated. How deep can you be if you only talk about "what's up"? No one talks about feelings, and if you do, then you're accused of thinking too much or analyzing too much and it's just a bunch of psycho babble anyway.

Kevin doesn't understand that I discover pieces of myself by talking it through. I'm not a human doing. He thinks I have to stop talking and start doing more. Well, who is he to make that claim? He doesn't know the work I'm doing, what it's like. He still seems to think it's about maturity and responsibility because he keeps saying it's time to "grow up". That just hurts a lot because it has nothing to do with that.

Maybe I do talk too much but I'm just turning to the wrong people. You do it for a good reason. As a result, you feel rejected, worthless, misunderstood, and you punish yourself for it. Recognize that this is a trap for you. You gravitate towards people like Kevin and then try to get them to understand you. It's insanity. It doesn't work. Do not ask for something that you are lacking.

Give yourself what you would like to receive from others. If you want to be seen a certain way, then act like it. You're an actress! Be those things. The only perception that matters is your own.

3/1/99

I'm not feeling great about myself. I'm feeling ugly and naked. I'm still upset about Kevin's perception of me. He thinks I'm an attention-getter when all I'm seeking to be is understood. I wanted to share the inner depths of me. No one else in this family seems to explore his or her emotional world, with themselves or with each other. They just talk about events. I consider that to be so boring. I seek to be more than just an outer surface. I'm struggling to connect both worlds.

What bothers me most about Kevin is that he presents himself in such a way that he can't be wrong. Why do I apologize? I'm entitled to feel differently and it doesn't make me wrong. It shouldn't surprise me; we're never going to have a heart to heart conversation. We don't have that kind of relationship.

Kevin doesn't listen, he just tells you what to do. Recovering from an eating disorder doesn't work in such a military fashion. What does he know about this? He has no experience with therapy or what it's like. I'm sure that he's never picked up a book or attempted to understand what I'm going through.

He intimidates me and makes me feel nervous. I am not my confident self around him. I question all my feelings and intellect around him. He's just like Dad, whom I feel the same way about. And they're like that because they never discuss feelings or show their vulnerability. It seems like they have no respect for people that do, or stop to consider that each person has an individual way of handling things. It is not right to judge that.

I keep talking because it keeps me alive. I do it for myself and I do it to help other people who are struggling. It's unfortunate that Kevin doesn't have an appreciation for that.

3/2/99

My worst fear in life is not fulfilling its purpose. I'm thrown off by what people say way too much. How do I get that iron will of focus and determination? This process of getting back to my *self* is going at a turtle's pace. I don't want to live my life for other people; I want to live my life for me, and only me. That's not a SELFish thing, it is sacred and holy.

On resuming Acting:
I think I want to do this but I'm going to take it slow. I moved too fast. It was too much too soon. I have to treat this gently. I don't want to be hindered by this. I'd like to alter it in such a way that will allow me to use it as a healing device. Perhaps I can create a drama therapy class or have a comic relief show geared especially for people in recovery.

Don't let this die. You have known joy, and have felt electrifying energy, on the stage. I think there are answers there. A very talented, intuitive, expressive, and passionate actress lies dormant in me. You *know* whom you are inside. Do not be afraid. God has given you a gift. It is your gift back to God to share it with the people.

3/3/99
When people resist another person's dream, it's usually about fear. My family cannot give me a set of rules and directions for something they know nothing about. They also do not fully comprehend my strength and my eating disorder serves as a perfect disclaimer.

Jo-D said to me that a lot of people stay sick, because if they really got better then they would hear, "I told you so...if you had just listened to us six months ago, you could have saved yourself". They'll take the credit when they weren't involved to begin with. I am getting better and I want to keep making progress, and when I've really got a grip on it, the credit will be all mine. No one can take this away from me.

There will come a time when I accept that they're not going to understand me and that it will be okay. There will be no blame or guilt. It's just how things are. I need to learn to accept myself and that I am different from each of them. Don't bang yourself up for being different. Be your unique special self. Let them be them and don't be angry that they're not like you.

I think acceptance is one of my major lessons in life. I first need to accept my body because it's my home. It encompasses my spirit. It is the only body I have and how I treat it affects every aspect of my life.

This is really hard. It's important to remember that I am not my body. Another way of looking at the abuse is that it violated my body but not my spirit and not my soul.

I am at the starting gate now. I can win this race. I can win at the game of life. I can become whatever I want. What I have to figure out though is what is keeping me from doing that and ignoring what the family thinks. What keeps you from taking full ownership of your life and your dream? It's definitely about unworthiness. I do not have fear or anxiety about the dream itself. I know I can do it. It's just that when I get started these demons reemerge. I could deal with that by it self but it becomes more complicated with the addition of the family "noise".

3/6/99

I had a fun time with Karen tonight. We got together at 3:30 p.m. and departed at 12:30 a.m.! That's nine hours of gabbing.

I remembered a lot of good qualities about myself. I'm inquisitive, insightful, curious, spunky, and sparkly. I challenge the system, I push the envelope, and I go to the edge. I'm loyal, caring, and true to my word. I don't depend on alcohol to be more sociable. I believe in my values and adhere to them (for the most part). I'm open most of the time. I try not to say judgmental things. I love books and exploring the human psyche. I'm always seeking to know more and be more. I never want to stop growing. I always want to be learning. Discovering new things is what excites me and makes me happiest. And I love good conversation.

On Mom being "worried" about me:
3/9/99

I'm feeling pretty good and secure about myself. I'm eating regularly and that still takes adjustment. It kind of pinches me and detracts my sense of worthiness when she sees something that is not there. She believes me though when I assure her that I'm fine.

Mom and Allen didn't get home until after 7 o'clock. I hadn't eaten yet and I could have decided not to. I was a little hungry. I told Mom that usually I wouldn't have felt good about that. I would have skipped eating altogether.

Something is blossoming for me. Oops, could it be? Could it be that...I...feel happy?! Now my level of discomfort has turned to pleasure. I am so happy because I don't want to starve anymore. I'm still scared about my weight, whether I'll stay the same or gain some. But I think I'm okay with not losing. As Jo-D said, "wispy no more".

I think I can trust myself. I know I can. Needless to say, I don't feel ugly today *or* fat. As I feel more connected and peaceful inside, the less those externals will seem to matter. It would be lovely and sweet to be in love with *myself,* and my body and eat without guilt. I can trust myself with finding the right balance with food.

3/10/99

I can still feel happy at a smaller scale. I imagine it can be exhausting to be on a high every day. Maybe that's why I feel tired.

In therapy, discussed my newfound happiness, and the triggered concern for Mom. On a sub-conscious level, she's worried because she only knows how to deal with me when I'm sick. I'm finally on the right track and I'm finding my way.

This isn't going to be the Celestine Prophecy. Before, their misplaced concern would trip me up. It would reel me in but not now. I feel strong and deserving.

3/12/99

Remember that every day is a new day and your body will have different needs. You'll put yourself through unnecessary stress if you forget to recognize this. Do not be scared off by your appetite. It will level out.

My work philosophy:
3/13/99

I'd rather be in a very positive environment embarking on

something I hadn't planned, to doing what I thought in what can be a nasty cutthroat atmosphere. I like to keep the attitude that the job is really a freedom that enables me to follow my interests. It's all in how you perceive it.

Most people feel unfulfilled because they define themselves by what they "do". The first question you ask a new acquaintance, or an old friend is, "what do you do? Or what are you doing now?" Why? We define ourselves by our work. Even in the obituaries, we're remembered for what we did rather than *who we are*.

That's why most people feel like "losers" because they're either not sure or are in a down-and-out job. God, we have to change our focus! We shouldn't have jobs, period. It's what divides us and keeps us unhappy. Instead, we should do what we love and share what we've got for everyone's profit. The "pay" back will be a harmonious and more peaceful world. In this world, there is so much energy directed towards solving problems and ending struggle. It's amazing if we can accomplish anything! I pray for wisdom. I pray that our world will progress to a higher emotional place.

3/15/99

I spoke with my beloved acting teacher, Katie, on the phone today. It was good. She was very pleased to hear that I'm doing much better. She said I sounded like I had "blood in my veins". I'm not comatose! She said, "we need you here (on the planet)".

I got a call for an audition for an independent film! What a pleasant surprise. It's come along at a time when I want to start kindling my interest again.

3/16/99

I had a feeling today that I wanted to throw myself into acting. I have moments like that when it overcomes me. I just want to pursue it with free abandon.

3/24/99

In therapy talked about my struggle with body image. I'm metamorphosing between anorexic and healthy thinking. One day

I think it's okay to be a little bigger and then the following day I see these imaginary bulges on my body.

Adolescence was traumatizing. I did not like my body developing. I've never felt comfortable with a sexual body. I've noticed that my bust line has returned and I want to cover it by crossing my arms. Additionally, I never wanted to have my period. Sex was not discussed openly in my family. Mom handed me a book when it was time for the birds and bees story. She told me if I had any questions, I could ask her, but how would I know what questions to ask? Her handing me a book only indicated her discomfort to me.

Right away I interpreted sex to be embarrassing and shameful. I wasn't encouraged to celebrate my body and delight in its every function. No one told me about masturbation; that it was a natural impulse and certainly not an immoral thing to do. It was acceptable for boys but rarely discussed or encouraged in girls. Not until I was in acting class did I hear people discuss their sexuality so openly. I had to figure everything out on my own.

3/26/99

I have continued to feel happy and content. It felt so good going into a group in a different emotional place, to see how much I've progressed. Each person is at a different stage in her recovery. One member wasn't there because of hospitalization. Another person left the group because it wasn't for her. And yet another member isn't sure she wants to continue. I recognized that I was perhaps the most advanced in recovery. I could see where I had traveled and that, indeed, I had moved from one point to another. It also feels amazing to know that I'm looked towards for inspiration. I have that glow about me.

4/15/99

Now I'm moving into territory where the struggle becomes internal. Externally, it's not as prevalent but all the questions and obsessions are still milling in my head. Should I eat or not eat? Do I purge or not purge? Yet, in spite of all this I still have to conduct my life.

When you first developed the eating disorder it met and satisfied a certain need. However, as it progressed, it no longer

Counting Bones

fulfilled that need, and became its own entity. I'm not even sure what that need was because it has been long forgotten. Moreover, I've never conquered this part of recovery. I'd panic and go back into the behavior. It's much easier to focus on behavior than it is to focus on the real issues without the behavior to distract me. This time I really want to do the tread work.

PART II

The Transition

4/20/99
    Body image is my struggle right now. I feel really overwhelmed with my body. Trying on clothes is an ordeal. I'm still small but I've filled out in all the places that used to be flat and hollow. I feel so bodacious. I hate it.

Reflection on growing into my body:
4/27/99
    The fear is, if people get to know me then they're going to know my story, which is always a risk.

In the aftermath of the Columbine Massacre:
    The presence of God is so apparent. The community already seems to understand the divine nature behind such a horrific event. They know that God is here. They accept that the children are with him, safe and at peace. I thought of that as the reason why this may have happened. The wake-up call is that we're lost and we're lost because we've forgotten God. I think there is a BIG link between violence and the elimination of God's name from public settings. One girl died because she professed her faith. She knew she was going to die. She wasn't afraid to state what she believed in. She gave up her life. Even when her life depended on it, she refused to deny her faith in God. I hope more is written about her. That was so incredibly brave.

Question of the Day:
5/12/99
    Why should they (my family) have the luxury of having the power to lead their lives and I don't?
    In therapy, we talked about my role as Power-less. My family will support me forever surrounding the eating disorder. What would they do if I got a full-time job, my own apartment, was active in theatre, and had a social life separate from them? There's an investment in my being dependent.

My thinking is different. It is my nature to analyze and think. What I think about doesn't enter their minds. I can still "make it" without them understanding me. I don't think like them either.

Combating creative stagnancy:
5/13/99

The question is how do I live my life and still have a life to lead? The answer is realizing that: No one creates like you do, No one writes like you do, No one acts like you do.

Thinking towards independence and empowerment:
5/23/99

You gain discipline through action.

Focusing on my role as a magazine consumer:
5/24/99

I want to cut back on anything that makes me feel less than worthy, one of them being magazines. It helps to understand what their target is. Most magazines are hypocritical. A majority of the headlines on magazine covers deal with diets, how to please your man, and how to make yourself more beautiful. For the most part, I don't feel all that great when I put a magazine down. It feeds into my body hang-ups and keeps me fixated on a fantasy. If I have that great lipstick then I'll feel beautiful and confident. It's okay to have beauty items but only to enhance what you feel good about, not from what you feel unworthy about.

On the irony of getting better, my family continues to see me as sick:

Mom pushed me about eating again and I told her that her approach didn't help me. She says it is so obvious that I don't eat. Or I go into my room. All I eat is junk food. Why can't I eat healthy food? Why can't I sit down with them? I play "games" with food. How can I go out on my own if I'm not healthy? Blah, Blah, Blah. Oh, and she told me she couldn't go through it again. Go through what?

I'm healthy. The doctor says I'm healthy. I've done a lot of work. I'm a lot healthier than a year ago. I've come a long way.

It's a big discount to me when they just pick on me about eating when eating is not the issue.

Mom says that she deserves to come a long way, to retire, and to not worry. I told her that I do not inflict this upon her. If she makes this her issue, it is something that she has to deal with. Her saying that she doesn't want to go through it again is hurtful because I *always* have to deal with it. She makes it sound like I do it on purpose.

6/1/99

I endured and survived another weekend alone. I figured I would work. Initially, it didn't bother me at all. I wasn't prepared for the depression that set in. It was really difficult. I felt confused, scared, and lonely. I couldn't make sense of it. I was mad, too, for the way I was feeling. It felt like I was coming undone. In a lot of ways, I felt like I was right back where I had been a year ago. It seemed so real.

I started to feel like I was going mental and believing what other people were saying that was untrue, such as having a problem again. But I've been doing so well and I've realized a lot of things. I came away from this weekend with more options and choices. Next time when I feel like this, I can have more faith that I can get through it.

6/16/99

Yesterday I felt really discouraged with the direction of my life. I just don't feel satisfied with just going through the motions. I feel this yearning for something more. I still feel like I should be acting. But I would be doing it, wouldn't I, if it meant anything? I wonder what is really authentic with my fascination of Hollywood.

Sometimes I feel like I have clipped wings. I can't fly but I can still walk. It takes me longer to get to where I want to be.

The eating disorder is what I have. I want to be able to say that I don't care. I'm not going to worry about it anymore. I'm going to eat what I want, when I want. I'm going to do what I want! I want to let go of my fear about everything.

I'm just really confused because I haven't been in touch with my soul and higher spirit. What I'm really afraid of is that I'll never be happy. And I'll be alone. The eating disorder is a form of maintenance right now. I have to get clear about what I want in order to have the bravery to extinguish the eating disorder.

On making my way "out of a paper bag" in the unfamiliar Providence, RI:

6/19/99

I feel great about navigating my own way. I didn't give up and go home. I found what I was looking for. This is exactly what I needed to feel relaxed and peaceful.

6/24/99

I hit a crisis point last night in which I felt suicidal. I just kept thinking that if I didn't succeed (committing suicide), then I'd have to deal with everyone's anger. I didn't do as well as I thought on the postal exam. It affected me more than I thought it would. It just feels like I haven't gotten anywhere. I felt angry, frustrated, alone, and eventually, plummeted down into the danger zone of hopelessness and worthlessness.

After talking with Jo-D, I realized I was in despair because I felt invisible, that no one really knows what I'm going through. No one recognizes my strength or courage, and I'm tired of this battle within myself. On the other hand, I don't feel courageous knowing that there are people who really are battling for their lives and some don't win. I'm angry with myself when I choose to be negative instead of positive.

Points of Anxiety for an Anorexic
Crowds
Food Courts
Time Constraints
Noise/Distractions
Stress

What she means when she says, "I'm not hungry":
I'm tired
I'm angry   Please help me
I'm lonely
I'm sad

6/25/99

More stimuli set me off and I'm starting to lose control. I'm throwing up more, even if I've only eaten a small amount. Either that or I feel really nauseous after eating, which just makes it harder to eat.

7/11/99

I understand the connection between feeling fat and wanting to lose weight, with feeling hugely dissatisfied with the apparent lack of direction in my life. It is approaching mid-July and I can't help but keep re-visiting this time last year. I'm still living at home, I can't go anywhere, (the car went to car heaven) I don't know how I'll work without a car, I don't have a job, I still have no social life or outlets, and I still have an eating disorder.

7/28/99

In the past week I've declined dramatically. I can't eat. On a "normal" day I take in 800-1000 calories. I'm supposed to be striving towards 1300, and that is just the minimum amount for my body to function. My nutritionist, Stacey, tells me I wouldn't even gain a pound until I reached 1600 calories. The eventual goal is 1800-2000 calories, and once I level off, I can maintain at around 1500 calories.

However, instead of increasing my calories, I've taken a dive, only taking in about 400-500 calories at best. I kept thinking, "what do I want to do?" Do I keep this to myself or do I call for help? Talking about it doesn't necessarily make me want to activate change. But I know how fast this can undertake me, and I don't want to be back in the hospital. I'm seeing Jo-D tomorrow and I moved up my appointment with Stacey by one week.

I know that in times like this, I need to have a plan to rely on. Eating the same things leads to eating nothing at all. Part of the struggle is an indifference to food. Nothing seems to interest me. The longer it takes me to decide what to eat; I am more likely to skip it altogether, just out of sheer frustration. I think a way to alleviate this is to have sample meal plans to follow, so that the decision is made for me. Just pick one and eat it. Soon enough, my body will start to connect with my brain again, and I'll know what I want to have. Right now, I think I'm not hungry and that's why I'm not eating. It's a distortion, but in reality, my body is hungry and malnourished. I have to do what I don't want to do to feel right: EAT. I just kind of have to put myself on Automatic Pilot. I just have to make myself eat and not think about it. This is why I'm seeing a nutritionist. It's just so hard to put eating back in order by myself. I can trust Stacey and what she tells me. I just don't have the objectivity to deal with food by myself.

7/31/99

I hate how I feel. After crashing this week, I'm now focusing on rebuilding what I've lost. I have to get to a place where my body can at least function. Yesterday, I consumed less than 200 calories. Today, I skyrocketed to 1100, still falling short of the desired goal 1300. Although I don't feel as foggy or tired, I still feel scared about my weight. This morning I felt an immediate lift after eating a small breakfast of yogurt and berries. It made me feel better which boosted my confidence. I thought, "I can do this" but now I'm back in the "I don't know". I'm tempted to cut back again tomorrow.

Sometimes I feel like I'd rather die than go through this hell. I put myself here and now I can't face the arduous task of making my way back. My fear is, "is this all there is?"

8/4/99

After therapy, I realized again that I can create and uncreate any circumstance. I can fight to be well. And the question is, why isn't health, by itself, enough for me to want to be well? I have to probe into not feeling deserving. Every day I have to think of why I want to fight. I have to build my strength in believing that I am enough. I am worth the fight.

8/6/99

Looking at old photographs triggered something in my brain that I had sort of buried and forgotten. I know what I'm afraid of. I'm afraid of my body betraying me as it had been betrayed years ago. I cannot feel good. My body cannot feel good. I think food and sex are very closely linked. Both are a substance of life. Both have turned poisonous for me because I was introduced to a world of guilt, shame, and secrecy. I cannot have the forbidden fruit. Bad things happen. Of course, being sexually abused, at some points, was not abuse because it felt good. I was sexually stimulated, and as a 7, 8, and 9 year-old girl, how do you deal with those feelings? Well, when you turn 14 years old, and you start to feel sexual, and your body is changing and getting out of control, you instinctively know to shun food. Stop eating and your body will lose its will.

A moment of clarity:

My body did not betray me. *He* betrayed me. My body is my friend, and my ally. Feeling good was a natural instinct and not my fault. It was his fault for making a good feeling feel bad. I can feel good again. I can feel good about sex. Food is not a poison. That is a lie that the anorexia tells you.

8/9/99

What do I do when I can't go to sleep and it's too late to talk to anyone? Well, subtract three hours and call whom you know in California.

Spoke to Kate who just returned from a 2-month trip to China. She was shooting a movie and also doing dialogue coaching. Her daughter, Chloe, is going to France for a year. Maybe she'll adopt me as her daughter for a year!

She said I sounded really peppy, which I don't really know how to take, because I'm skirting thoughts of suicide. There is no mercy with an eating disorder. There is no act of euthanasia. No one to put me out of my misery. And if I do it, what will become of me? Will God forgive me?

Sometimes I think I'd have more impact in heaven than on earth. And the only place where I'd know complete happiness and peace. When I was born what did God intend for me? Why was I born? What am I supposed to be doing? I feel like I am way off the mark. It would bring me tremendous relief just to experience a few moments of heaven. If I could visit God there, the angels, and Nana, and then I could come back if God wanted me to. I feel like a life-altering experience is necessary.

Counting Bones

Author's Note:
These thoughts were a result of the continuing media scrutiny of the growing trend in Hollywood for actresses to resemble "lollipops" (becoming so thin that the head appears too big for the body) and the acceptable size to be had dropped to ZERO.

8/18/99
Why am I so fired up about this? The anger I feel is what results from still having a dream. I'm angry because it doesn't seem fair that I'm not a part of the club, and I think I can play my anorexia to somehow retain my rightful territory. I'm not like everyone else. I'm special. I've mastered one major element of being successful in Hollywood, which is being thin. All I have to do is show my talent.

The goal is not to waste away. I can put on weight and still be very thin. I need to eat to feel strong and happy. It helps to deal with the ups and downs of life. When you don't have adequate nutrition, the low times are really low.

I can be in therapy for months talking about family issues. I think I'm waiting for family to become perfect so that I can leave, so that I only have the road ahead of me. But if I get on that road, the family stuff won't have as much power. I'm still letting them direct me. I am the director of my own life. You're seeing yourself through their eyes.

They'll never say, "OK, go for it". This is my dream, so respect it. The years go by fast. I don't want to be 40 years old and sad. I haven't made peace with letting go of the dream because I don't want to let go.

8/20/99
I was thinking to myself last night that I need to transfer all the energy that I focus on keeping small, into honing my dream and talents. I've done this to myself too many times. It's too painful to recover the steps back to health. It will be worth it and I'm never going to plummet again. I'm giving my scale to Stacey to take away from me. I think that is a crucial step to get my obsession off of numbers. I never want to know what I weigh. There's no reason for me to be concerned (unless it's too low). I

can be weighed in once a month but it's information I don't have to know.

I just want to live my life and regard my body as a wonderful machine that allows me to run, skip, dance, taste, smell, feel, and have fun. There are people who are paralyzed or die, and both know that it's not the gravity of the body that matters. It's the expression of the body.

My hand allows me to write. I can feel connected to paper. There are so many things to be grateful for that are taken for granted. I want to be alert. I don't want to be sleepwalking through life. I want to find life and life to find me. There are two ways of looking at the world. It can be rosy or it can be bleak, and both ways are true. Your perception is your reality.

9/8/99

It is no coincidence that my creative well has run dry. I've been half-dead for several weeks. I didn't want to write because life had become uninspired.

Interlude:

On September 2, 1999 a significant and frightening event occurred that would force me to make a life-altering choice. That morning I was standing in the kitchen, having a discussion with my mother and step-father when I felt all the blood draining from my head to foot. Navigating my way back to my bedroom proved unsuccessful. I didn't go two feet before my feet crippled beneath me. Everything I grabbed onto was like fine sand. Everything was muffled and distant like I was underwater. I could feel my mother hugging me and crying softly into my shoulder. I wanted to comfort her. I could feel myself being carried to my bedroom. My mother was sobbing as she tried to dress me to get me ready to go to the hospital. In the background, I could hear Allen frantically calling 911. I lay before my mother not knowing if I was dying. I wanted to say, "I'm sorry. I'm so sorry". But I couldn't find my voice. I was still semi-conscious. Later, I would find out I was under for ten minutes. The paramedics came and took me away in an ambulance with my mother beside me, and Allen following in his car.

At the emergency room I was given the routine blood tests, blood pressure, pulse, and orange juice. I didn't even want the juice but obliged under the circumstances. After a few hours, when I was deemed stable enough to go back home, I was given a pacemaker with instruction to wear it over the next 24 hours to monitor my heartbeat. When the ordeal was over, my heart wasn't endangered, but wearing that machine must have knocked some inkling into me that this wasn't normal. As my nutritionist soberly told me, "healthy people don't go to the emergency room".

I thought I had to be at death's door to finally make a decision to be well. And suddenly I realized I was at that door. My body was a ticking bomb and I had no idea when it would go off. What if I was driving? I could kill someone or be in an accident that would leave me in a wheelchair, and what would I do then? Everything became poignantly clear. Suddenly it became very urgent to take action, to get my life back, because I didn't know how much time I had left. It was in this moment that life became precious again. I wanted to be alive. And so it began, after years of starts and stops, that I became convinced that this, indeed, would be the turning point. I would never come back to this place, this illness, again.

The First Day of my New Life Begins on this Day Forward

9/9/99

I was really emotional about eating today. It didn't feel like a victory to me. I felt remorseful. I felt angry. I felt grief.

I cried most of the night because the world, as I know it, is ending. I want to make good on that promise to myself. I never want to experience what I felt yesterday again, although I'm not sure if the 1st day towards recovery is the hardest. I think the 2nd and 3rd day could pose a challenge. I have to keep going.

I don't know how it is that one day I just roll up my sleeves and pick up a sandwich. I don't know how I did it. I didn't WANT to do it but I'm accepting now that I NEED to do it no matter what. I've been waiting to feel okay about this and I've recognized that it's just not going to happen. I'm going to hate this process for quite some time and that is an appropriate feeling. Therefore, it is the act of acceptance that is enabling me to eat. I'm accepting that I will die if I don't eat. I'm accepting that I will hate eating and that my body will change. However, I also know that it will pass.

Just as it was startling for me to engage in eating so abruptly, so it will be when I cross to the other side. That will be the day when I wake up and know that I've done it. The hatred, torment, and guilt that I have felt will melt into acceptance, peace, and joy. That is when the NEED will become the WANT.

It is like I am raising myself from the dead and this will be my resurrection. The devil, in the form of anorexia, will never tempt me again. It is ironic that what I believed was my torment is the thing that will make me well. My fears and distortions will balance out. I have to see the connection that when I eat, the obsession with food, weight, and numbers will dissipate. I will *gain* control, not lose it. I need to realize that eating IS control. It allows me to handle issues in my life much more effectively. Why make life that much harder to live? You can't starve yourself and expect to live; whether you physically die, or not, is not relevant by itself. You can live your life for years and be emotionally and mentally dead. To me, it is synonymous.

What is really happening is that I'm having an out of body experience. It's like the part of me that seeks to be well is stepping outside of this body and watching me go through the process. That spirit is coaxing me along and telling me it will be okay. It IS okay. I will step back into my body when I accept this truth for myself; when spirit and body are in synch with each other. It will come to pass that I will understand and accept that I am much more than a BODY, that my body has certain limitations.

9/10/99

My head feels a different kind of dizziness; it's swarming from all the food I'm eating. I feel kind of intoxicated. I hate it. It is day 3. If I stop now, then all the pain and grief I've felt will be invalid. I'll have to start again and it won't be any easier. I have to stick through this.

I feel ashamed of my weight going up. I don't know why. Each time I go to the doctor, I'll be a little bit heavier. I'm afraid.

Counting Bones

9/13/99

Yesterday I threw out my scale. I had weighed myself that morning and it read 103. I decided that I didn't want to watch the numbers go up. It's not necessary for me to know.

Every day I have to think and act in that of which I wish to become. Weighing myself is not part of that behavior. I want to focus on how I *feel* rather than how I look. I want to stop thinking of myself in terms of numbers. I don't want my days to be affected by my weight. I want to concentrate on how I would like my day to go versus debating what foods I should eat. Food helps me to live but I don't want it to rule my life.

Weighing myself became a habit. Having a scale just prompts you to hop on. It affects how you live out your life. It limits you in what you can do and offer. Parties, weddings, showers, and holidays will always overshadow any fun you might be having.

I want to live with free abandon. I want to love life. Thin is not beautiful. Spirit is. When your spirit is alive in all its wonder and curiosity, then you are beautiful. When you feel enthused, and your eyes are sparkling, and your cheeks are flushed, then you are beautiful. What is not beautiful is starving yourself into an ashen coma; a world with no choice or freedom.

Celebrating your life and your spirit should be embraced, not erased. You deserve to feel beautiful. It's not from what you eat or what you weigh. All externals are counterfeit. It's how you see yourself inside that reveals your external truth.

A struggle worth enduring:

It's going to take time for my body to adjust. It's going to take time for my emotions to settle. It's important to remember I'm trying to break an ingrained habit. It's going to be hard work. It's going to feel uncomfortable. But it's worth the effort. I just think that if I give up now, then I have to start again, and that was already too painful. I don't want to go through that again.

Fighting Strategy:
9/20/99

In my calendar I place a star for each day that I do not purge.

On overcoming temptation after a meal out with friends:
I almost left early so that I could purge but I knew staying would be far more beneficial than having short-term relief. My discomfort passed after about an hour. If I had gone home, I would have just been alone, and it would have set me up to fall back again the next day.

9/27/99
In the past few days I've been wishing for the comfort of my anorexia. Can't I just have it for a day? The "voice" tells me I've been doing so well, how will one day hurt? But I can't allow myself that satisfaction. That temporary relief is fleeting. It will only tempt you to seek that feeling more and more.

10/01/99
I see the connection that my life is worth living when I eat. My life meets me rather than me running towards life. When I don't eat, everything shuts down. The world comes to a stop. It cannot enter my being and it cannot receive my energy, so nothing happens. And even if I'm thin, it doesn't matter, because I'll never see thinness for what it is. When I'm thin, that's all I have. When I'm living, I have everything.

I need to understand that pain, loss, and disappointment is just as glorious as joy, laughter, and contentment. That's life and life is really good when you're accepting it rather than fighting it. It works with you, not against you.

Interlude:
In the midst of my life taking shape, I experienced another extraordinary event that reinforced the universe meeting my choice of life-affirming action. I never mentioned that my friend Khristian and I had an estrangement. After she came to visit me in California, I realized that we were at very different places in our lives. Rather than confront this openly and honestly, I chose to burn a bridge. I didn't think I would ever see Khristian again, and how would she ever forgive me? Well, the good Lord made it known to me that he would mend that bridge, when I literally crossed in front of Khristian's path one day at the mall. As it goes,

I ordinarily wouldn't have been there. But it was right after a harrowing therapy session, the kind that makes me realize what I should be doing and I'm not doing it. I had no idea what to do (emotionally), so with lack of anything better to do, I head to the mall rather than home.

Khristian saw me first and called my name. When I saw her, I almost died. I thought, "Oh, no! You know now". What that meant was that she didn't know I had come back home from California. I felt humiliated, embarrassed, a failure. At this point, I was still supposed to be an actress and Khristian had been one of my most loyal supporters. What would she think of me now? What I hadn't credited to Khristian was that she was also my most loyal friend, even when I thought we weren't friends anymore.

She came over and hugged me and told me how happy she was that I was home. It was a mystical moment. It seemed like time had never passed. The hurts and misunderstandings just seemed not important anymore. I learned in the year and a half that I had last seen Khristian, she had a baby girl and was engaged. She was to be married on October 3rd. It was August 25th when I saw her, and before the emergency room incident.

What's special about Khristian is that she readily invited me back into her life without question, and knowing that I was obviously very sick. She invited me to her wedding, only six weeks away, and went to immediate work at playing matchmaker. She taught me a lot about forgiveness and being a friend. It helped me to be self-forgiving. Going to the wedding also gave me a formidable goal to get my life on track. I wanted to enjoy it. I wanted to thank Khristian by taking that act of measure. It paid off. I went to the wedding, caught the bouquet (much to Khristian's delight), and met a match in Khristian's friend Gary. It was a really sweet time. I was acutely aware had I not made a decision about my health, that none of these things would be happening, and so I kept going...

On a Romantic Blossom:
10/5/99

I know I'm with the right person when I don't feel scared, that I'm pure rather than damaged. I'm dazzling in spirit. I'm shimmery. I'm beautiful. I radiate love and truth. This is who I am.

I knew this moment would come, I just didn't know when. To me, this is a really big landmark because meeting Gary shows me that I was able to open my door. He was able to come through. Moreover, I wouldn't have seen Khristian either. I haven't felt in synch with God and church lately, and for not feeling totally connected, God has really shown himself to me. My life is amazing. There are still a few things I could change, but for the most part, I'm still flabbergasted to be reunited with Khristian. God works through people and I'm so grateful to see the light.

The struggle to adequately nourish myself continues:
10/8/99

I've been kind of gauging my success by how I'm following The Plan (my food plan). I've been struggling and focusing on the plan, and what I'm *not* doing. This just promotes negative feeling and feeds into helplessness.

Talking with Jo-D last session, we addressed how to be prepared to recoup especially during vulnerable times. Instantly, you want to react the way you reacted before. It's second nature. I can learn a new way of responding to my immediate environment.

On the evolution of my relationship with my mother:

I can see her not just as my mother but as another woman who is struggling with her self-worth. I kept wondering "why?" Why does she put up with it (Allen's drinking)? And then it hit me: she doesn't feel deserving.

A part of me wants to talk with Mom. I'm allowed to feel concerned about her just as she has been with me. She's not happy. She can't be. When I come home and I think she's mad at me because she doesn't greet me with the usual peppy hello, I'm beginning to realize that it's not me. She's alone and partly because she put herself there. I understand what that's like.

I want to know what happened in Mom's life that made her feel undeserving. When she was young, she was spirited and mischievous. I still see that sparkle when she's around her girlfriends. It's a real treat to see this side of her. She's a playful and fun person with a witty sense of humor. But somewhere along the line, something or someone, threw a wet blanket on this exuberance.

It's just getting worse, his drinking; he's drinking more than he is not. I think he's sicker than his daughter (an alcoholic). I know this is horrible to think but I hope something does happen just so that he can see that he's a drunk. I'm afraid that's what's going to happen because he's never going to own up to it. It used to be that you could play off the drinking by making it into a joke but now it's just blazingly obvious. It's embarrassing.

Everyone can see that he's not a normal drinker. When he drinks, he becomes belligerent, stupid, and utterly disgraceful. That's how I can see that it's worse because the alcohol has seized his personality. It doesn't help him to be sociable and charming. That ceased years ago. Now he's a drunk who does not have control of the alcohol. It has turned him inside out. He's not Allen anymore.

On anticipating the First Date:
10/10/99

This feels very uncharacteristic because I've been so afraid of intimacy in the past. The thought of someone touching me would make me feel sick. Now I'm anticipating physical intimacy. I don't know what I'll feel in the moment, what will transpire, but I feel excited to feel this desire. It is passion. Feeling physically aroused makes you feel alive. I think why it feels different now is because I feel deserving. Therefore, I'm not afraid to feel sexual. My fear has become a non-issue. I think it will be more about pacing myself, and what I'm comfortable with.

A questionable change in eating presents obstacles:
10/12/99

I recognize that I'm waiting to feel hungry, and as I'm waiting, my body is shutting down. I don't feel like eating. But if I don't eat, the less likely I *will* be able to eat. I haven't noticed that I don't eat, but other people have definitely noticed.

On tabloid publicity, media sensationalism, and my role as the Consumer:
10/14/99
    I want to limit my exposure to tabloid publicity and media promoting unhealthy images. I've been aware of the connection between those images and how I feel, but I haven't eliminated them from my life. I want to do that now.

    What led to my decision was the cover of this week's People magazine, asking the ancient question, "When is Thin too Thin?" and featuring emaciated actresses, as the subject of concern. First, to think that People magazine is actually concerned about the welfare of these actresses is grossly estimated. That magazine will sell and it will sell to the very population that is caught up in the obsession with thinness. The article does not promote healing. It's very empty-hearted. It does not serve the purpose of awareness or enlightenment. It is the tumor of this sickness that's eroding the minds of those affected by it.

    I don't want my mind to be eroded by it. I'm not picking up another magazine that promotes objectification of women. I don't want to be concerned with beauty products. I want to read about life and culture; things that feed my brain not starve it.

    I am a consumer that chooses not to consume the hypocrisy of the media.

Experiencing physical intimacy is still unfamiliar, unsettling territory:
10/16/99
    I know what Khristian means now when she says, "your body will tell you what to do." I can't wait to share more than just abbreviated kisses with Gary but it's a weird sensation; this feeling of desire, of wanting more, of *feeling* desirable.

10/21/99
    Addressing these issues in therapy. I was telling Jo-D that this dating thing is confusing because I don't have a compass. This is uncharted territory. How do I know what steps to take and when? How do I proceed to reveal who I am? How do I know

what's real and what is from past wounds? The part of me that feels damaged is what's raising these questions.

Khristian advises me to just let things happen. Communicate what I want and don't want. Emphasize that it's not personal. You don't want to send personal messages.

I think I will give it a few more weeks. I want to give him a chance. I want to know for myself that if I decide it's not working, that I'm doing it for the right reasons, and not because I'm avoiding uncomfortable feelings.

Thinking about venturing out on my own again:
10/22/99

My life has been very active and full. I have more and more control of my life. I'm not as attached or as needy of the home front. It's something that I feel peaceful about. Mom and Allen were there for me and now I'm strong enough to venture out on my own again. Most importantly, I don't feel scared. I don't have any doubts in my ability to carry on with my own life. I'm not going to be plagued with troubles. I feel the freedom of living my own life. It's not a struggle. I don't think I'll return to that state. Life always has its struggles but I've triumphed over this one. I don't feel the same desperation. I'm not fighting just to stay alive. I'm alive and it's wonderful. I'm alive and I can endure. I know that nothing can break me. I can rise above any occasion. This is what this illness has taught me.

10/25/99

I'm calmly flipping out over my body. I'm trying to focus on the positive such as how much stronger I feel. I don't feel weak or dizzy. I'm not consumed with hunger. My attention span is longer. I'm not as tired. These are all good things!

10/26/99

The reason I've been flipping out is because I've been doing really well; there's an undercurrent of the need not to be well. It's the illness saying, "hey, wait a minute..." I'm still very cautious of that voice. Actually, I'm more conscious than not. Not so long ago, I couldn't even distinguish that voice. That's how entangled I was. I didn't know how to get untangled. It seemed impossible and hopeless. Now I don't feel out of control. It's still hard but I'm managing. I'm aware of everything I put in my mouth. I want to reach a point where it's not on my mind. I trust that will happen.

Things present themselves when you're not looking. Things pop up. Everything is moving along and I'm not suspicious of it. I'm grateful and I'm happy. They are miracles. I think, finally, that the worst of the eating disorder is behind me. Even Jo-D said that she didn't see me returning to that place.

I'm feeling more comfortable with myself. I feel much calmer and peaceful. The world seems to be inviting rather than menacing. I awake with a smile rather than a sigh. It's still a process. I'm not denying that there still won't be other hard times, but I won't be dealing with them through my eating disorder.

It's true that an eating disorder is an act of cruelty. It becomes more unfathomable. It won't become possible to commit such an act against the body. I didn't deem it possible to stop purging but I'm doing it! I've almost completely eliminated it.

On relationships and sexual trauma:

I'm feeling uncomfortable with Gary. I haven't seen him in a week. I turned down an invitation. I don't know how to talk to him about what I'm dealing with. I've been feeling ashamed. I'm not comfortable with certain bodily contact. All I want right now is to kiss and cuddle and nothing heavier than that.

I tried the make-out thing because I have thought about it in my head and was curious. There is a first time for everything. I discovered I didn't particularly enjoy it. I didn't feel connected. I didn't feel like myself. However, it may be that I'm not allowing myself to relax.

11/14/99

It's kind of a weird sensation: I feel thin and fat at the same time. I'm aware of both worlds of delusion and reality. I'm aware of each step I'm taking. It's like half-and-half with me. I'm still very aware of the sickness. It's still a day-to-day process but it's not like a fight. I'm matching every step to the illness so that I'm just keeping steady. I'm not feeling desperate. I don't feel alone. Every day I still think about what I'm eating. I still have thoughts of

NOT eating. The difference now is that I'm not acting on those thoughts.

On writing and how it keeps me alive:
11/22/99

A large part of writing is to help me remember the tyranny of an eating disorder. I have to remember how horrible it is to be at the bottom. Yeah, I feel uncomfortable with my body and eating but I have mental clarity, I'm not fatigued, and I'm much happier. I have to keep moving forward. This eating disorder path is just worn to death. You cannot cross it. It will not hold you up. You can walk away from it. You really can! It's going to take a long time to feel completely over it but it will happen. Don't get discouraged.

On the splendor of recovery:
12/2/99

I love the ordinary daily tasks of making my lunch, washing a dish, writing a check, etc. Every moment seems significant because I'm doing it for myself. It's my freedom that feels so special.

On the decision to Tell:
11/30/99

It just reached a point where I felt it was time to lay my cards on the table. Either we have something or we don't. I can't venture into certain situations if he's not aware of my issues.

And dealing with the Consequence:
12/3/99

Gary decided he doesn't want to date right now. I'm not taking it personal. This is exactly the reason why I told him in the first place. Either we have something or we don't. And for me, to go any further without revealing some truths about myself would not have felt authentic to me.

I know that I want a partner in life, not just a playmate. I did the right thing. I followed my instinct to tell him about myself, and my answer is fulfilled. He's not ready so it's better to move on. I've learned something.

Interlude:
After the Thanksgiving holiday I ventured out of my mother's home and into an apartment, sharing with another woman who had advertised a share at work. Although I hadn't actively been seeking an apartment, when I saw the ad, it seemed like an opportunity, a natural step in the evolution of recovery. I felt confident and healthy enough that I could approach this change of status to independent living without trekking backward.

12/20/99
I love what I do. I love who I am. I think about who I was and how it seems like, my life before, was like trying to communicate under water; the sounds and images were all muffled. Everything around me was distant and far away.

People relate to me different. I'm my own separate entity. I'm not an extension of anyone. I'm not in the middle of the hubbub. It feels so good.

Surprisingly, I spent the whole weekend at Mom's house. It's really weird because now that I have a choice, I don't feel as anxious to go.

On dealing with life in time of sorrow, after the passing of Allen's mother Esther:
1/11/00
I woke up feeling restored and peace had replaced my burdened heart. I had to go through last night's grief, but now at this hour, I'm feeling exhausted and depleted again. It was a killer day just because my whole system was down. It's difficult just to speak. Talking all day is so tiring. It doesn't help matters that I'm not eating properly. I'm so tempted to take a day of rest but that feels so self-indulgent. The world continues on even if I don't feel like it.

1/12/00
I so much want to take a day for myself but I'm resisting it because it seems inappropriate. Unless I'm laid up in bed and can't lift my head, then it doesn't seem proper to call in sick.

Jo-D encourages me to take a day if I can afford to. There's nothing wrong in doing that. It may feel self-indulgent but it's not. It's OK to take time for myself. It's OK to feel the loss. It's necessary to feel the grief so that I can move through it. Taking time *is* professional because it allows you to rejuvenate and come back refreshed and focused.

When it's more than just grief:
1/16/99

I did decide to take a day off from work. Instead, I went to see Jo-D, where we discussed feelings of undeservingness and how and why that is. The session was laborious as I spent most of it contemplating rather than talking.

I still felt lonely and sad when I got home later at night. I felt like there was more I was dealing with than just Esther passing away. Then it did come to me. It's like time stood still as my subconscious became conscious. The sexual abuse occurred during this time of year. The snow, long dark nights, being sick, feeling lost and confused. It's so simplistic and yet so loaded.

1/29/00

There was a time that I described the abuse as being shattered into a million pieces, and how in the world could I fit all the pieces together? What I felt was deeper than empty. I felt a perpetual sadness that wouldn't lift even on a sparkling sunny spring day. I felt removed from the outside world. I have always felt like I've been on the outside looking in. I've never been able to fully participate and let myself go.

I don't really feel pain so much anymore. I feel like I've put the pieces back together. I'm much more familiar with whom I am and I'm able to distinguish what I'm feeling. However, I still feel guarded. I still live in a world of gray shades. What I anticipate is to paint my world with brilliant colors, adding orange, yellow, green, and red hues.

A reaction to a too-thin family member:
1/31/00

It was alarming to me when I first saw her. I squelched the nudging question because I didn't want to give attention to it. I know I hate being asked that question. But the anorexic in me was like, "no, that's not fair. You can't do that! (be skinny)"

I called her with the intent on getting "the skinny" of why she's so skinny, but in the end, it was meaningful to talk about what's real. What matters is not why she's so skinny, but connecting with her. It's really none of my business to know. What I do know is how *I* feel when people scrutinize me on the basis of my weight. People can't assume what's going on in someone's inner world. It's unfair to make a negative assumption without having any information to base it on. All I can do is take care of myself and not let her thin appearance influence how I feel.

2/2/00

What will keep me committed through this difficult time is that there is no avoiding. The way I cry now is different because it's not from a place of despair. After a little over a year of taking the medication, I feel like I've reached a significant point where it has done its job. The depression is lifting and what is coming forward is real. I've gone underneath all the layers of depression to reach what is real. What I cry for now is kind of joyous, because it's like I've found myself, and it's not so bad.

2/8/00

In therapy, talked about the meaning of success. I'm trying to understand. I'm not afraid of success. I can picture how I feel. The problem is I don't believe I'm successful now. It feels like a choice I have to make between my family and myself. However, it doesn't have to be that way. I can live my life and still be at their level. They don't need to support or understand what I do. When you stop feeling like you're being judged, and that you don't have to apologize or explain why you do what you do, that you only have to please yourself, THEN you can really move forward. But believing in yourself is a verb. You have to exercise your faith continuously. It is never over.

2/23/00

It is important to be mindful that I'm in control. I can change the dissatisfaction in my life. What I feel good about is that I'm not falling back on my eating disorder to fill that void. When I have felt vapid, I would use my eating disorder to feel validated. It was something I was good at. It gave me a false sense of power. However, now I can stop myself and see that it only strips me of all power. I will not let it con me.

I've resisted wanting to be thinner by repeatedly asking myself, "what good did being thin bring me?" I have to be here. My body feels so heavy but I still weigh only 105 pounds- still skinny by medical and societal standards.

I have to re-examine what my goals and priorities are, what I'm selling short on, what I need to do, etc. It just doesn't do any good to be unhappy. If you're not happy, then change it, but be gentle in the process.

4/6/00

One thing I'm enjoying is working out. It makes me feel really good and more positive about my body. It helps with everything; mood, attitude, eating, sleeping, etc. It's much better to feel strong and fit than to be a withering string bean. Yet, I still feel sadness and I don't know why. It's as if someone died. As I move further away from the anorexia, when I see pictures or videotape of myself, it's like watching another person. I think about this coming summer when we go to Saquish and how much fun we're going to have. I look forward to playing games and being athletic. I look forward to eating a hotdog.

Last year, I didn't eat. It's such a horrible feeling because you want to be there, you want to be there with your family, and instead you distract yourself with a book. Or you clean up the kitchen while everyone else eats. And you know deep down what you're sacrificing. You don't know how to be there. Even when you try, you just want to jump out of your skin. The people around you are trying to engage you and lure you back, but you're fidgeting, thinking about what you're not eating and the roll of fat on your tummy. It's too painful to sit still, too much, because you know that if they lure you back then you might lose control. For a moment, you may stop caring and take a bite of food.

Sometimes I still regret ever taking that first bite of food. It changed everything. But where would I be if I hadn't? I can't think about it. I can't go back. I have to focus on what I have now. I'm doing so much! I feel great. It's so good to feel great.

Interlude:

For most of my life I have always been keenly aware of God and his greatness. Even when I was being sexually abused, and in its aftermath, I understood that he would be my salvation. I never went through the struggle of "is there a God?" and "why me?" In that respect, I was very fortunate, because it meant I always had hope. I knew there was a reason for whatever I was going through, so it gave me the strength to keep trooping forward. I knew there was a plan for me, for any one of us, so it wasn't up to me to just quit. Yet, for all my efforts, for all my pleas, and meditation, I still could not get this monkey off my back. I didn't want to live the rest of my life weaving in and out of an eating disorder. I didn't want to settle for that. I had to wonder what was missing.

Although I had grown up Catholic, and therefore Christian, I hadn't been living by God's word. I hadn't really let God in. I hadn't given my heart to him. I knew about Jesus, the cross, and resurrection, but I didn't quite believe that I was included in this sacrifice. I wasn't worthy. No, God hadn't called me by name. Now I can see that, throughout my life, he has been calling my name. He has wanted a relationship with me even more so than I had with him!

It doesn't take an earthquake or some equivalent staggering event to give your heart to the Lord. The heavens didn't open up, and I didn't feel much different, but four days after my 29th birthday I made my commitment to Jesus and wholeheartedly accepted that he did die for me. That's what was missing in my life. As with anyone, a person cannot come to you unless they're welcomed. More so, it is very difficult for someone to help you, when you're not willing to hand over the reins. I still wanted to be in control, and the conflict is, God is in control. Life is so much smoother when we allow God to lead us. We're the ones who get in the way.

The only thing I hadn't done up until that point was to surrender myself to God. I recognized my human flesh as severely limited. I couldn't battle this alone. I've often described this battle as a spiritual warfare and it is! But I had to come to a full awareness that indeed, I was worth fighting for, and God had a legion of angels ready for me. God was just waiting for me to say the word.

4/14/00
The world is different today because the angels are singing for me. Last night, Jena (my cousin and also a Christian) and I prayed for God to take this struggle away from me. I don't want it anymore. It's familiar but I don't want it. I don't want it to be a daily resistance. I want it gone. It's spiritual warfare and I can't fight this demon by myself. The angels have surrounded me with their shields and swords, and I feel the peace and divine intervention of the Holy Spirit. This morning, I woke up with a big smile, because I can feel God's presence. It's such a wonderful feeling.

Experiencing frustration in the workplace:
4/15/00
Even in the midst of despair, I'm remembering that I'm not stuck in any situation. I am in control of my life and I have the power to choose. It's important to maintain responsibility, to resist temptation to walk away. What will sustain me now is making the decision that I will not stay in this situation, and moving towards something that will replace it. Walking away may have short-term relief but it is not a wise move for the long-term. Having something to walk to is a much more empowering thing.

On experiencing a shift, a disconnection in writing:
4/25/00
I think part of the difficulty is what happens in the aftermath of an eating disorder, or any obsession that takes up most of your life, for half of your life. What do I write about?

It's a strange relationship that I'm beginning with myself. It's still me, but it's like an awkward silence, nervous and self-conscious, not feeling good at anything I do. I could never do anything so accomplished as starving myself to death. A large extent of my writing was about this accomplishment, but let's not play a broken record. It is time to create a new melody.

4/27/00
I've decided the way to make it through this writer's block is to discipline myself to write, even if it's about nothing. Waiting to be inspired just doesn't work its magic. I have to write to be inspired. It's easier to write when you're emoting. The challenge comes when you've gotten through all that stuff, and it's tempting to go back, just so I'll have something to write about, but no, it would just be incredibly boring. The subject is very tired, it's not interesting, and I have no use for it anymore. There are much more lasting, joyous, and fulfilling ways to discover who I am. I don't have to be a tortured soul to be riveting. I am shifting the way people have perceived me. Yet, I still think I'm fat.

On the realization that I can contribute to the field of eating disorders:
5/7/00
To think that everything I went through has been a gift is just incomprehensible to me. I am now certain that I have crossed the threshold. I am now able to administer.

5/16/00
Sometimes I still freak out about hunger. It's not a shattering feeling anymore, like I want to cut myself, I can't stand it. I still hear the "voices" but they're more distant and detached. I try not to question my body's hunger signals. My body will tell me what it needs and how much. It's okay if I eat more on some days. It's not okay to malnourish the body and feed it less than what's required for peak performance. You need muscle to be strong and function properly.

On remembering who I am:
5/19/00
This is my life and I have choices of how I want to live it. I want to become more centered in my internal philosophy and become less bothered by outside opinions and perceptions. It is up to me to be happy and to create my happiness. What makes me happy is expressing my passion.

5/23/00
    Most of my unhappy moments that I can think of have been attributed to traditionalist regime. I don't like traditions. I resent being expected to conform, and even though no one can stop me from making my own choices, it certainly hasn't been a comfortable place to be in.
    I'm thinking of being brave. I'm thinking of letting go of what everyone else thinks. There are people out there who will admire my non-traditionalism. There are people out there who can inspire me.

5/31/00
    I feel some happiness and wellbeing as I prepare to nod off. Although it's still a daily struggle with body image, I feel a little bit of an accomplishment that my body is healthier and stronger. It's weird to recognize that my bones don't stick out anymore. I'm still thin but not emaciated. However, gaining weight has not meant getting flabby. My process has been very gradual though. I think it's been less traumatizing that way versus being in a hospital, where everything happens at once. Yet, I really haven't sat down to think about all this.
    It feels great to move, jump, and lift. It still takes courage to continue this new lifestyle despite the tremendous benefit. It's still hard to let go of the stick-thin ideal. It's weird to look at my body changing. The results are exciting yet peculiar too. Whereas before, I measured my success by the width of my hipbones, now I can account for so much more beyond my looks. I feel content, peaceful, and a satisfied tiredness that accompanies a good day's work. There are so many things to be mindful of.

Continuing to grow in Christ:
6/15/00
    I'm becoming more fulfilled in God's word and understanding. I've had great moments of joy because I can see what I couldn't before. I'm learning about patience, love, and gratitude. Everything is in its proper place.

Fighting to withstand a loveless job:
6/18/00

My lesson in this is to be patient and not bolt at the first feeling of discomfort. Another lesson is to be grateful for what I have. There is strength to be had in waiting. It builds character integrity.

Everything is as it should be. There is a time for work and for play, a time for joy and for sadness, everything has a cycle. Happiness is not stagnant. No one can be happy all the time. Would I want to be?

Do not say anything. There is more strength in quietness. Do not rebuke those against you. There is freedom in compassion. The minute you begin to fight is when you have given up your power. Know who your adversaries are.

I'm not going to give in to my weariness of this job. I must focus and be mindful that this job is temporary. I must still do well at my job.

Do not live for the weekend. Make every moment count. Create room for your spirit and passions every single day.

A Precaution when the Red Flag goes up:
6/29/00

So much has been going on inside my head and I have a peripheral view of how it affects me. It's like watching a home movie of myself. I'm aware of what's happening outside of me at the same time that it affects me on the inside. That, alone, is a huge growth because I can deal with things as they come.

I've felt the temptation to starve myself. I've felt the familiar pangs of loneliness and depression. Right now, I'm alone, while everyone is still out at the beach. It's hard. I came home and I purged. I haven't purged for weeks. I knew what I was doing but I had to do it anyway. I didn't have to. I was making a choice. I did feel relief afterwards but I also know that it's not a solution. I do know that this is my weakness. This is my weakness that comes up when I feel lonely or depressed. But it's not something that has to swallow me up. Damn this disease, that I would allow it to pull me under. No way. No way.

My world is different now. I've felt angry and under-appreciated. Those two feelings have distorted my vision. I'm entering a sensitive time period because at this time, for two consecutive years, I fell ill. Both illnesses occurred during spans of alone time. The time alone didn't instigate it but it's like a lion on prey- the illness waits for your vulnerable spot before pouncing.

Déjà vu is not a reason to become sick. I'm stronger than that. Moreover, déjà vu is only as powerful as you make it to be. Some circumstances may seem similar but I'm not anywhere near where I was emotionally one and two years ago.

I'm much more fit to fight back. If I'm feeling depressed and lonely now, it's not nearly as bad as I would feel if I lost twenty pounds. There's no reason or rhyme to it. If you go down that road, you're going to die, and that's all there is to it.

Now I have a relationship with God and that means everything. Human beings have limits but not God. Therefore, when I feel disappointed or angered by people, I must hand that over to God. He's the only one who will never forsake me. He understands my faults and weaknesses. I can go to him with anything no matter how much I repeat myself. He is a loving, compassionate, and just father. I need not be afraid. In fact, it's worse trying to hide, which is nearly impossible because he's all knowing. However, that's what's great about him, he is ALL KNOWING. He sees what I cannot see. He sees what's ahead of me, what my reward is, if I'm patient and obedient to him. So now, it is anguish to me to wait on this job opening up- but he knows and will take care of it. He also knows what happens when I take a detour, and by his grace, I can feel him nudge me, I can hear him in my thoughts, when I'm tempted to go down that road. The nudging is gentle but never controlling. The choice is still mine.

That gentle nudging and guidance reminds me of Cassandra. We had to repeatedly guide her away from "no-no" spots. She would keep going back no matter how much we re-directed her. Sometimes, it wore on our patience, but she is a baby who is curious.

I sort of see myself like that with God. I'm still a child who will impulsively dive into things against my best interest. Most of the time I'm conscious of it and sometimes I'm not. But God is holding my hand. Like a child, I am never out of his sight. If I fall down and bruise my ego, his arms are always open for me to run into.

I didn't have this knowledge a couple of years ago. I knew God existed but I hadn't come to believe that Jesus was my savior. I knew he was THE savior but not personally for me. I couldn't believe he gave his life for me; on the cross, he knew me, and would be my strength and light.

A fighting strategy:
7/1/00

Remember that Cassie and Cailin love their Auntie Michelle. Don't you dare go back.

Changing the way I think about numbers:
7/12/00

I was feeling a little bit fat today because my clothes are more fitted. My thinking is changing because rather than change my weight, I'm changing my size. Normally, I'm a size 4, but a looser fitting size 6 feels more comfortable to me. So that's what I'm going to do. It's ridiculous to try and reduce. I don't need to lose weight. I look and feel good, and I'm not going to feel any other way. I'm never going to be a size 0 or 2 again. I'm slowly making peace with that fact.

When I accepted a new job, I took two weeks off, and the anxiety I felt was unexpected:
7/23/00

I've been aware that with feelings of dissatisfaction, obsessive thoughts have lurked in my head. I found myself counting calories, both in my head and writing them on paper. I felt guilty about food choices. I even entertained the idea to purge. Even so, it still felt different from where I've been in the past. I felt at an arm's length from people, whereas before, I was totally immersed. I couldn't be around anyone for lengthy amounts of time. Additionally, no one would have noticed a struggle going on as they once did. Although I was debating whether to eat more, it looked like I was just taking my time eating, which is normal.

I feel gross about my body too, even though I'm still skinny by most standards. I don't have an ounce of weight to lose and no one would ever think that about me. These feelings come up when there is a space of time. It gives me something to do. But I don't want to do it. I don't want to feel this way.

7/24/00
I feel good about myself because I have more to offer. People can appreciate my company because there's more of me to give. Before, I used to get aggravated and frustrated because I had earned people's pity. However, the less healthy I was, the more limited people became in what they could give me. All the gamut of emotions narrowed down to pity. But now that has expanded to a much wider range.

On going to church and realizing, when you take one step towards God, God takes ten steps towards you:
8/1/00
I've noticed that everyone has come up to me! That is definitely God's help because I haven't felt brave enough to approach people. It's been an effort just to show up. But now I can see the reward of making that effort. It gives me faith to keep showing up. What would I be doing at home but most likely corroding my mind with television?

The message was about Jacob. He wrestled with God and asked God to bless him, even though he had received the promises and blessings already, and he had wealth, twelve sons, and two wives. Yet, he wanted to hear God's blessing HIMSELF, and what God did, was grant him a new name Israel. The question to the church was have we wrestled with God?

I think I have wrestled with God when I beseeched him in my struggle with anorexia. If I had let go of God, I wouldn't have survived. I asked him to bless me and he ended my struggle. Now what I pray for is bravery to help people and guidance through the publishing of this book. I know that my book is in God's hands. Whatever anxiety I feel can rest in God's hands, because the need for it is so overwhelming. I'm not worried anymore.

8/6/00
      Just when I think to myself, or state out loud, that I don't see myself having a problem with eating again...it happens! But I suppose there's a difference because even if I slip, I'm able to stop again, and get back on track. Additionally, I immediately recognize what I'm doing. Although I feel bad for the slip, I can feel better for picking myself up and brushing myself off from the incident.

8/16/00
      In therapy, discussed my concern with Mom's pending reaction to my book. I'm worried that she'll be hurt by some parts of it. However, that's what it was about for me, and what this whole process is about. I'm not that girl anymore. I went through that to get where I am now. Mom has to appreciate the struggle. I endured, and what was then, no longer applies today. She may have issues but those issues cannot affect my own process. We can still work through those issues.

      To make this easier to transit, I have to become more comfortable and accepting of my recovery. Then I'm okay with however the family reacts. This is what I went through, this is who I was, and this is where I am now. It's all-cohesive. I can't omit the uncomfortable parts because that's feeding right into the shame and secrecy, which I'm fighting against.

      I also talked about Kevin and how angry and hurt I am by things he has said and not said. Jo-D surmises that he's not a giving person; how he acts is a protection of his cool and machoism. He doesn't think about how he affects people. He hasn't made a connection that I'm a changed person. I am going to find ways to initiate changes and to be able to let go of my hurt and anger.

Reflection on marriage and partnership:
8/18/00
      I know that my Lord and my God loves me, and even though I've only recently given my heart, he knows that I've been earnest and seeking obedience and faithfulness my entire life. We experience trial and error to gain maturity. I endured, and one of the things I held hope in, was that I'd eventually find someone

who would love and cherish me, as I would in him. I learned to stand on my own. By standing on my own, I don't look for someone to hold me up, but rather to stand *with* me.

Marriage isn't about filling an empty part of yourself. It's adding to the whole self, and what you already are. I no longer feel broken or incomplete. I don't have these lingering questions that hang in the air. I made it through to the other side, and now I'm ready to share my life with my husband.

I feel so happy. Yet, I noticed old worries and nuisances emerge today. I felt preoccupied with my body and food. Wouldn't it come up for me a day after I pray for my husband? To make such a commitment further transcends me above the eating disorder. An eating disorder can take on the face of a lover. It is far riskier to be in a committed relationship, but the rewards are indescribable.

Still adjusting to my body image and size:
8/21/00

It's hard for me when people who don't know me, comment on my small stature, because they have no idea how subjective it is. I'm learning to offshoot it, to just throw the comments off my back. I'm adjusting to my size and training my eye to see what's really there. I can be slender without having ribs or hipbones poking out. I guess I'm at the point of what most people would deem "perfect". If I gained 10 pounds I would still look good, but if I lost 10 pounds, I'd look sick.

I guess the next question would be, then, why not gain 10 pounds? And my answer would be, my mind wouldn't be able to handle it. I think I'm doing very well where I'm at, and as long as that's true, then I don't see anything wrong with weighing 110 pounds. I'm not in danger. I'm healthy. And I'm eating.

8/22/00

This morning I was getting a large steamed milk (trying to get more calcium) and the lady didn't give me the correct change. It reminded me of an example Jo-D brought up about worthiness. There's temptation to just say, "the heck with it", and then be irked for the rest of the day. Or you can speak up for what you deserve. It's your money and you deserve the correct change back. Some people just don't want to go to the trouble, thinking it's a nuisance, but what's that about? When it concerns you and what's right and fair, there is no trouble. Even the bible doesn't tell you to just give away your money. It doesn't tell you to sacrifice yourself into wimpiness. It's all for self-empowerment and strong principles.

Later on:
It's been a strange battle today. I've felt so fat and the urge to avoid eating is strong. I was walking during lunch and I just thought that the only way to shut up this "voice" is to eat! So I ate half a sandwich and it seemed to settle at the base of my throat. I wanted to throw up. I did better than I planned though because I ate the other half during break time.

It didn't turn out so bad but the fight isn't over. It's similar to someone embarking on a fitness program, and in the excitement, will buy new workout clothes, sneakers, and any other equipment. Just the same, I want to get all my equipment like a calorie counter and a scale, and I have to tell myself, "NO!" I can't let this torment me again. I won't let it.

On presenting my book and publishing pursuits to my mother:
8/28/00
Mom was really gracious about it and thanked me. She seemed to understand that it would take courage for me to let her read it. I told her it would be difficult at times, but to remember that I'm in a different place now. I also want her to read it from beginning to end while maintaining an open mind. She said that she would.

I began by affirming that I loved her. She got a little emotional when she sensed what I had to say was nerve wracking for me. She took my hand. That gave me courage to continue.

About five years ago I had left my journal unattended by accident and Mom took it as an invitation to read some of it. I had been so upset because in no way would I have wanted her to read it. It was such an invasion of privacy. Therefore, it seemed appropriate to present it to her in this way. Now I'm *giving* it to her. I want her to see inside of my soul. She has my permission, and hopefully, will understand things she hadn't before.

Now, of course, I'm apprehensive as I wait for her to read and finish it. I hope she's not too hurt by things I wrote about her. I will have to keep coaxing her back to the present moment and remind her that I love her. Just as I am a different person, I recognize that in her also.

I want this to be a blessing rather than a curse. This is such an opportunity to heal and grow, to have an open discussion, and to shed understanding. I'm hoping this will allow us to grow closer together. I think that we've moved beyond those hurts and limitations. It's not a time to argue or become defensive. What I went through was very real to me, and however she reacts, it doesn't change how I felt at the time. It's time to ask questions and seek insight rather than taking defense. I pray that God will allow that to happen.

9/5/00
So much has happened this week and I experienced such a wide range of tumultuous emotion. It is the first day over the last week that I'm starting to feel like my normal self. I felt guilty, sad, burdened, angry, and overall devastated because I hurt Mom with what I had wrote.

Talking to Jo-D has helped me through it. I didn't intend to hurt Mom. What I wrote was during the very moments of my illness. I brought them to light because I think I can help people. Mom will come to understand that. Opening all this up is very fresh, very real, and painful. I've been dealing with this all along, so it's going to take time and patience, for Mom to come to grip with all this.

My faith in God is helping too. I have faith in people because God works through us all. I'm not supposed to turn my back. I have to stand still and just wait. I always have to keep my focus on God and let him guide me. I can't devote myself to the flesh or earthly matters.

Reflecting on the drama of a gifted child:
Every family has an identifiable person who struggles the most within the system. There's this homeostasis that needs to be maintained, and I don't even know how that is determined or by whom, but because of circumstance and my nature, I became the

person who was squelched for speaking up and taking a stand. In turn, I wouldn't tolerate anyone trying to diminish my observances. I wouldn't take "No, this is the way it is". That was just unacceptable to me. To do any of that would require me to give up some part of myself that I cannot tolerate.

The person to become the anointed scapegoat of the family is the one who is more intellectual and sophisticated. The very being of that person challenges the less developed members of the family to look at issues that they can either choose to ignore or just cannot comprehend.

When Mom reacted the way she did, it was feeding into this old scenario. It made me second-guess myself. It's like a hook reeling me in and I can't take the bait. I can't fall back into my old position of "eating disorder". I have to keep living in the present.

There is honor in what I have written. You have to go to the deeper layers to see the beauty. When I was writing it, I had no foreshadowing of publishing it. I was trying to save myself in the only way I knew how: writing. And now, when I look back, I know that I can save others by letting them be a witness to my writing.

PART III

The Complete Surrender

9-12-00

For about a month now I've been locked into an old ritual of checking my image in the mirror. When I get up, when I go to the bathroom, when I go to bed. I'm aware that I'm doing it and I acknowledge it. I tell God, "I'm doing it again!" I have to stop because it's not healthy. I've been feeling fat and thick. I used to be able to clasp my hands around my ribcage, and I know that sounds really gross to think about, but because my fingers don't touch anymore around my waist, it just feels huge.

My eating is back to normal, pretty much, after having a tough couple of weeks. I feel confident now that when something like that happens, I can snap out of it. When it's happening, it can feel like you're back to where you were, but you're not, just because you're not the same person. It's sad in a bizarre way. It's a hollow feeling to acknowledge that the sickness is gone. That's what I learned from this. I learned that I'm stronger, and even in my weakest moments, the sickness will never seize me. I won't drown in it.

I've been astonished by acts of faith this week. I'm supposed to be doing something good for Mom just to show my appreciation of her faith in me. However, she turned that around, and took me shopping at her invitation. It was really nice. Of course, what I picked out was put away for Christmas, but even that was good because *I* picked it out. She wanted to get ice cream afterwards and the least I *could* do was treat her to that. The following morning, on Sunday, she told me she would go to church with me sometime and to "not give up" on her. Later, my cousin Kevin (and Jena's husband) told me he had been praying for both of us.

Changing Relationships: Jo-D
9/13/00

I woke up with an ungrateful heart. I'm trying to snap out of it! Mostly, I'm troubled because I feel unsettled with Jo-D. It would have been OK, if in the last ten minutes of session, we didn't launch a discussion of church and Christianity. At first, I wasn't going to elaborate, but I did when she prompted me. Thus, I told her about being Christian and of the time Jena had prayed for me and the miraculous results. There is a defining moment when one door closes and another opens- and you just know that the struggle is different. I'm not alone. I don't think anyone can overcome a struggle on sheer act of will. Man cannot do it alone.

Jo-D wasn't directing this at me, but she said she felt leery of people who said stuff like that, that they found God and therefore, never craved alcohol, cigarettes, or what have you, again. It suggests that the responsibility is off them. However, people from the outside, (of this world), wouldn't understand what this healing experience actually means until they've experienced it- the "it" is the Spirit of God. There are two points to consider. First, you don't *find* God, He finds *you*. Second, you begin to understand the difference between what you can do and what God can do. The difference is you're no longer holding the reigns yourself. It is so much easier when you just allow God to lead you. Quite frankly, I'm surprised and disappointed that Jo-D doesn't get this, but I shouldn't jump to a conclusion, because the conversation isn't over. That's what upsets me most; it's just a huge, heavy, open-ended topic to leave unfinished. Now I feel all this uncomfortable stuff and I have to wait. However, I am curious as to why I feel angry and defensive? Is it natural to feel that way? I feel judgmental and that's not supposed to be Christ-like.

Later on:
I called Jena during my lunch break and she helped me process my confusion. Feelings of anger and defense are just a normal response of being human and it can be frustrating when someone doesn't understand what you're saying. There could be a few possible scenarios, but however it works out, I have to bring it to God and let him guide me. Maybe I won't be able to talk to Jo-D about this and I need to go to a Christian counselor or maybe this is an opportunity to be a great witness to her. Maybe she needs to hear what I have to say.

It was really encouraging talking to Jena because she affirmed all these changes in me. My whole look, attitude, what I have to say and how I say it, is completely different. The world isn't about me, my problems, and how I'm affected. My mind has broadened and my whole outlook on life has expanded. I have a sunnier disposition. Jena says I've grown dramatically and realized things that have taken years for other Christians to know. But I think God has always given me a special ability to understand, and it's just been lightening speed, once I decided to accept him.

I'm so excited about what God is doing for me and wants to show me. I'm so grateful for Jena and the church community who have been witnesses to me. If they can see the changes in me, then it's got to be evident to my family. I know Mom has seen it. I know God is working through me and touching her heart.

Taking the next step in therapy:
9/22/00

I just returned from seeing Jo-D. At first it was weird and awkward because I wasn't really clear on where I wanted to go next. She suggested using therapy as a practice forum for things I want to accomplish on the outside. She can be a sounding board or just support me. I guess I'm still figuring out how she will fit in from this point.

We talked about how I want to be viewed and how all these traits can attribute to different facets of my life. I've known that about myself. I don't have to be everything to everyone. That's a good thing to know. A lot of women struggle with that.

On finding my voice within Family Ties:
9/29/00

I hate feeling that whatever I do, I'm creating some huge sacrifice, whether it's at my expense or theirs. As far as the book goes, I think that if I publish it, it would be the end of my relationship with my family. Something seems terribly wrong about that.

10/7/00

I'm experiencing a transition in writing. I feel out of sorts because I'm emerging as a free individual. So much of my writing has been contained within prison walls. It reminds me of the prisoner who gains freedom, and then doesn't know how to function in the outside world, because he lost all contact with the realm of society.

Being bitten by the acting bug: illusion or reality?
10/14/00

Big things are happening, not in physical form yet, but I feel God is at work delivering me, preparing me, ready to open doors for me.

I've felt restless and dissatisfied; a yearning desire to expand beyond where I'm at in all aspects. And yet, I've grown tremendously over the last several months. Looking back, I can see where God has been, and now I have to believe he is still at work in my life and is leading me to where I want to go. It's important to remember that God will fulfill my desires in a way that will bring me peace. Right now, I don't feel peace because I don't think I gave acting a 100% shot. I couldn't. Although I haven't acted in a couple years, I have to give equal merit to the fact that I put the rest of my life together. Now I CAN act and be able to fully give that effort because everything is aligned. I don't have all these battles. It's a different place too, because I know the Lord. He can direct me now because I have a relationship with him and will listen to his direction.

I *did* receive an answer to one of my prayers. It came to me while I was praying again. It was a strange ominous feeling but now I believe I CAN hear God. I prayed for God to show me, lead me, tell me what he wants me to do, and to help me make sense of all these thoughts and feelings I'm having. I want to follow HIM and his desire for me and not of Satan. I want to know that it's God talking to me and not Satan.

Of course, the first thing I want to do when I feel lost or sad is to isolate. But I called Ed and Pat (a married Christian couple at my church that leads a weekly Bible study) instead, to talk to them before cell group, and it was great. They were very supportive and compassionate, and as I talked to them, I felt peaceful. They affirmed that I seemed to know what I want and had thought things out. They suggested I could even bring my creativity to the group.

Anyway, I was thinking about Ed and Pat in prayer and how wonderful it was to know them and everyone else I've encountered on this Christian walk. And then the answer came: "I'm laying the foundation". God is helping me build a strong foundation on which to stand!! Of course! You need to have a strong foundation to weather all storms, i.e. rejection, disappointment, discouragement, hopelessness, etc. He's preparing me for the real journey. I couldn't make it before because I didn't have a foundation. I wasn't patient and did all things according to my own will. But I can forgive myself because I didn't have a relationship with God to know any better. Now I know God and I'm learning to be patient, to wait on him, and be obedient. It's really remarkable. What an awesome, loving God.

10/17/00
I've been thinking more about this "dream" and what it means. It occurs to me that every time I "dream" it's when I'm feeling lacking. It's those times when I'm not feeling so good, not pretty, not funny, and life is either overwhelming or just dull. But this happens to everyone right? Everyone has a dream to escape.

I'm recognizing now that it's not the "thing" that I want but the "feeling" that derives from that. I need to learn how to cultivate the *feeling* into every day, more attainable, realistic goals and activities. I think about how relatively small the entertainment industry is; it's like a clique mostly, and such as it is in high school, it can seem downright unfair how some people can get anointed into this elite club. But- like high school- you have to grow up.

Interlude:
Right around this time, I had started a new job working in the customer service department of a travel operator company. It was essentially my first real job with benefits and salary that I had never reaped from temp work. It was a marvelous, liberating feeling. Yet, at the same time, it sparked insecurity and inadequacy as the job was quite demanding and not all of my peers, who were hired with me, were making "the grade". I was in constant fear of losing my job. Now that I think of it, it's funny that I hadn't put my trust in God (I'm still at this company a year later).

This was a miniscule factor in my backsliding but it did contribute to my taking the reins back from God for the comfort of my own control. Everyone has a weak spot that they revert to under times of pressure or stress. The mature Christian will know to rely on God. However, I was just a baby, only 6 months in Christ, and like a baby I wanted immediate gratification for the discomfort I felt. I went right back into the familiar patterns. Although I didn't see it then, it is clear now, that the following entries were to be a foreshadowing of what was to come.

10/31/00
I've been having thoughts of starving myself. It was really strong over the weekend. So far, I've been OK. I'm conscientious of eating but I'm not flat-out starving.

I wouldn't just stop eating altogether. I know enough not to do that. I can't shock the body. I have to trick it into thinking I'm still feeding it. So I eat, but I just change what I eat, and I spread things out so it feels like I'm eating more. Here's today's menu:
Breakfast: 1-cup brown sugar oatmeal
Snack: 1-cup low-fat yogurt
Lunch: 1 ½ cup salad with lite dressing
Snack: natural peanuts, approx. 30, 2 oz. turkey breast
Snack: 1 fun-size Butterfinger, ¼ chocolate chip cookie
Dinner: ½ cup applesauce

I was also living at home to save up for a new car and here are my thoughts on changing my attitude towards money:

I don't think I'm going to be a spendthrift after this because I know I have it in me to save and that I LIKE saving. It feels good knowing I have a nest egg. When I'm not spending money it forces me to go inward. I think about what money can and cannot do, and it can't give me a warm feeling inside.

11/3/00
Therapy was groundbreaking today; talked about what I brought up in my letter regarding my weekend in NY, work, and my resolution to starve myself. I experienced a moment where I really felt like my mind had "snapped" and all logic escaped me.

Counting Bones

Jo-D says there's an actual term for this, "instantaneous" something, but it's the experience of when your philosophy changes in an instant for no apparent reason.

She asked me to think about what I wanted. I told her we had talked about my wanting acceptance and respect the last time we met. But to go deeper than that, I think what I want is a piece of myself. She says I'm a step ahead by realizing that what I want comes from within and not outward externals.

This inward concept is directly related to how people see you. I think there is a gap between how I perceive myself and how the world sees me. It's not completely congruent. Although we agreed it would be a waste of my time trying to fix dynamics with each person in the family, what I can do is be loving and accepting towards myself. Part of that means speaking my mind about what bothers me. This gives an opportunity for people to understand me. This allows me to show who I am. For example, I feel hurt when Kathy or Chrissy asks for my aid with the kids but they don't really acknowledge my efforts. I also miss connecting with *them* when they push the kids on me. However, they don't know how I feel unless I tell them.

For the most part, it doesn't usually happen that people will finally "get" you and then act accordingly towards you. It's the other way around. When you stop caring so much about being understood is when they'll "get" it. By that time, it doesn't really matter, because you will have already accepted yourself.

I have to act on loving myself. This is how I'll find and keep a piece of myself. When you're depressed, irritable, or ungrateful it's because you've neglected your care and needs for days, weeks, and even months.

I want to keep a balance between internal and external selves. When they're equal is when I'm happy. It means I'm not sacrificing who I am. I have to say what I feel. That is loving myself, it's also loving other people, to be open and honest with them. Love isn't all happy and romantic. It can be really tough. It's really true that when you love someone you will let him or her go. You let them be who they are. And if they understand, they'll come back to you. And if not, it was never meant to be.

Spending time in scripture:
Matthew 24:36-51- The Day and Hour is Unknown
Jesus will come when we least expect him. We should always be prepared and act accordingly.

Matthew 25:14-30- Parable of the Talents
Man who puts his talent to use gains much; man who hoards it loses everything.

11/7/00
Today marked my 3rd month with the company but instead of feeling more secure, I feel insecure. I still feel like I could be disposed of. But you know what? I keep forgetting that God is in control. As a Christian, my life is supposed to be free of worry. Whatever happens, I have to believe God will take care of me.

11/8/00
I don't know why I resist reading the Bible so much or spending time with God, because when I do, it's so uplifting. I have been praying for Jesus to give me peace and in those moments, I can feel something. One time today I cursed his name and quickly caught myself. NO! Holy is his name.

11/10/00
Tonight I was surprised and devastated by thoughts of suicide. I know I've been struggling lately, but not until today did I realize I'm depressed again. In therapy today my energy was really low. I think I can only muster enough to get through work. On my days off, I'm finding it hard to care about anything, including myself.
I think what frustrates me is that I have goals and dreams for myself that have given me stamina to continue, like having a family of my own, but I begin to wonder when that will ever happen. Kathy and Chrissy have a shared blessing of being pregnant together at the same time and expanding their families. They have lives to live for. I don't feel like I have anything. I don't feel like I'm working towards anything. I don't know how to reach out to anyone. Who wants to hear from a depressed person?

It was scary to feel suicidal again. So I came up with something better that's like a dose of morphine. Starve.

On a logical level I know this is all wrong. It's hard for me to shake off this feeling. I really don't have the desire to. I've heard of people, who after making the decision to kill themselves acted happier, therefore fooling other people into thinking things were better. What really transpired was that the "decision" brought them peace. Wrestling back and forth with indecision is what causes misery. For me, it doesn't seem worth it to fight.

I felt like calling Kevin up out of anger, to inquire what was so selfish about suicide. What would he really miss about me? When has he ever shown me love? All he's ever done is ridicule me. I didn't call him. I don't care what he says about me anymore. If he does say anything, I will not hold back. It's time to tell him what I think of him. Who is he to think he's any better than I am?

The struggle ensues:
11/11/00

I've been thinking more about how I'm feeling and I'm thinking towards prevention. Isn't this what people mean about asking for help? Why do you let yourself get so far gone before you say anything? I have three options: I can kill myself, I can starve myself to death, or I can ask for help. If I go down this road, it will be my fault.

It's difficult to think about going on medication again but maybe that is what I need to cope. None of this white-knuckle stuff will do.

I've been looking at Cassandra's picture and she's the reason to make me continue. She would care whether I was around or not. Cailin too.

I wonder why some people can just be sad or depressed but not feel like dying and yet others do? But I guess it's the same as why some people become anorexic and bulimic and others don't. It's how you're raised and what you believe about yourself.

I don't know how all of a sudden I just need MAJOR help. How did this happen? I've been going to therapy all along. Even Jo-D says she overlooked any chance of relapse because I had gone such a long time without any sign of it occurring. It usually happens closer to the onset of recovery.

A Cry for Help:
For his anger lasts only a moment, but his favor lasts a lifetime; weeping may remain for a night, but rejoicing comes in the morning (Psalm 30: 5)

11/14/00
I didn't get a chance to write over the weekend since my suicidal episode on Friday. On Sunday I got a surprise phone call from Judy (a member of my cell group). I had no idea what to think because it was out of the blue. But I went over to her house to spend time, thinking that maybe she wanted to speak to me about her son who just got out of the hospital for depression. If it was that, I certainly wasn't in the place to offer advice or inspiration.

It was a couple hours before Judy said she didn't know why she got an image of me and a mental note in her head to call me. Then I knew it was God who had impressed upon her mind. He knew I was isolating and heading into denial. This was urging me to break out of my shell. It inspired me, but truthfully, it's still hard.

11/15/00
This is God. He is making me aware of what I need to do, the steps I need to take, and that I really am headed for relapse if I don't take those steps.

Relapse happens when you don't know what else to do. I think there's only a slight few that actually don't care and it's a definite "f*** you" to the world. But that little part of me that DOES care wants to fight. No, I honestly don't want to relapse, not when I have other choices.

The other choices would be to talk, get on medication, go to a support group if need be, etc. This would definitely be a sin to disregard these choices because then it would be deliberate.

11/18/00
I don't know what to do. I can't eat and I can't talk. I have to ask myself, "what is preventing me from eating?" And it's the *not eating* that's affecting my ability to talk.

I feel this shame that's feeding into this helplessness because I should know better shouldn't I? Yet, it doesn't feel like it's me who's pegging myself into this corner. It feels like an impossible unshakable force. Anyone else might tell me, "No, it's you and you alone".

It's harder for me to mask what I'm feeling inside. I can't pretend. I can't force a smile. My brain is already shutting down and I've only lost about 5 pounds.

11/19/00
I'm feeling more desperate. I had a glimmer of hope earlier today when I pondered what I would want to do in life and that is helping people who struggle with this problem. Yet I can't do that if I'm sick myself. So why am I doing this? It's so incredibly hard to stop. If it's this hard now, how can I expect it to be any easier later?

I'm also feeling depressed because I don't know how much more J0-D can help me. What I need help with, she can't help, and everything I need to know, I already know.

11/20/00
I visited Jena tonight and I left never addressing the original agenda I had which was to seek counsel on the struggle I've been having. Yet, I feel much better for not ever having spoken about it. I was talking about other things that were fulfilling, and I think it was a combination of being myself, sharing with Jena, and her sharing with me, and having that connection time. That's what gave me energy, and even as I was sitting there I was thinking, "I'm not depressed". It gave me insight that I just have to remember to do things that I care about and have a passion for and not get dragged down by the mundane things in life.

A decision to go back on medication:
11/25/00
 I've responded to this all wrong, relying on old methods and patterns of thought. Rather than taking control of my life, I'm taking control of my eating and it's all wrong. It doesn't solve anything. It takes away energy that I need to feel good, and even when the chips are down, I need my strength. It is especially important when I don't feel so good, that I need to be in shape.

The Relationship begins by deciding to turn my journal over to God:

Happy New Year
1/01/01
Dear God,
 I love you. I am so happy and grateful to know you. I want not just to know you but experience you. I only know about you and of you, and with exception to a few occasions, I've never quite known what it's like to experience your love.
 I want to be close, intimate, and comfortable with you but I don't understand who you really are. I don't know what you sound like, look like; I can't see or touch you. Right now I have a very difficult time listening to what you're trying to tell me. I don't know how to communicate back and forth with you. Teach me to hear you. Where do I start? How do I begin? I think you're telling me to read your Word. That was the first thought that came into my mind.
 God, I don't know why it's so hard to trust you. Well, I do, and I know you understand. I've never actually had a father figure, and what I had either disappointed me or betrayed me. You are my supreme father, and even though I had assurance that you were watching over me, it's still hard for me to let go and let you take control.
 I want to be totally devoted to you. I want to follow your best plan for me always. I know that anxiety should not register because you are sovereign. Nothing happens without your permission.

Counting Bones

1/9/01

OK, God, I haven't been in touch the way I've wanted. As always, you're in the back of my mind. I struggle with bringing you to the forefront. Yet, whenever I spend time with you, you're always right there making me smile.

God, what do you think of my illness? What do you think when I refuse to do what's right? But this isn't a moral issue. It's hard when I get entangled. Of course it's logical to eat but an eating disorder defies all reason.

OK. I'm not feeling anything. I'm not feeling any motion or stirring inside of me as to what you're trying to tell me. So, I'm going to go back to the scriptures. Guide me towards what to read.

1/22/01
Dear God,

Ed had a really nice message for me in prayer. He said, as he was praying, he saw this beautiful clear blue vase sitting by itself on a mantle, and the vision was supposed to represent me and you were pointing to me, putting me on display and the message was that you were proud of me. God, that was so reassuring to me! It made me feel so good to know that you see me in such a beautiful unique way and that you have confidence in me.

2/7/01

I feel guilty for neglecting you God. It's so hard to let go. It's hard because I'm dragging my feet. I'm fighting with my own will, not yours. With you God, everything goes right. God, I'm tired of feeling exhausted. I'm tired of not feeling good enough. I'm tired of this battle that I just can't seem to give up. I ask myself, "what's the pay-off?"

What gain is there in my destruction, in my going down into the pit? Will the dust praise you? Will it proclaim your faithfulness? Hear, O Lord, and be merciful to me; O lord, be my help. (Psalm 30:9-10)

Interlude:
On February 18, 2001 a very significant event occurred that would change the course of my life forever. For several weeks the church service message was building and it was as if God was calling me again and again until it was no longer something I could deny. The message was about not looking back and that there was an imminent breakthrough about to happen, but the miracle cannot occur if we keep turning our heads. Lot's wife only took a glance back and she was turned into a pillar of salt (Genesis 19: 26). God showed mercy again and again to the Israelites, and even so, it took them 40 years to cross to the Promised Land, complaining the whole way. They were still lured back to the "good old days" when they were in bondage. It is part of our human nature to forget about how bad life was before and not being grateful for what we already have. Since the days of Egypt we still want to talk back to God about what we think is best or it just takes us years to yield.

The message to me was clear, the time had come for me to step up and confess, but this was not to be a private confession. No, God knew what my strength was and he beckoned to me in a way I could not ignore. I just knew that if I left that church without yielding, I would deeply regret not meeting God. I had no idea what he was about to do but I had to trust him.

Thus, with great expectancy, I moved towards the front of the church and alerted the pastor that I had something to say who graciously handed me his microphone (the service had wound to an end). These are the words that I professed to my church, to my God, and to myself:

"I'm up here because I feel led to and I don't know what I'm going to say; I have an idea of what I'm going to say. I know the words will be given to me.

I can't tell you how I feel that God has been speaking to me, maybe to everyone, but to me in particular in the last few weeks. You may not know me, but you do know me, because I'm your sister. My name is Michelle and I am your sister. I feel moved to share my experience and I feel like God has been telling me that- it might not mean anything- but I'm beating around the bush here...I have to speak the truth and I need to hear the truth, and the only way I know how to do that is to just share what I've been going through, and the truth will set me free.

What has enslaved me for 15 years is an eating disorder. I've been anorexic/bulimic and it's all because I've been looking back to a big lie of... as a child, someone stole my body and what I've been struggling with, what I'm realizing now, is that it was a lie. God is my Father. That's what I want to say today. A year ago I became a Christian, but you know, there is a difference between having the knowledge and walking the walk. I've had the knowledge but what makes it so difficult is the letting go. Just letting God give you the grace to live your life, and so now I'm saying, I'm letting it go and I give up my body. God is saying, give me your body, I'll create it anew. I gave you a beautiful body. Stop doing what you're doing. What happened to me when I was 8 years old was a lie and that's my distortion.

So today, I just want to say that I claim my heritage in Jesus and I'm following God. I feel there's your individual body and then there's the Body of God and I'm joining the Body of God. Don't be focused on the past, don't be focused on people, just focus on God and let God do his work. I want to thank you, thank you God, thank you Jesus.

Just pray for me; by opening up now that I can stop lying to myself and start sharing the truth of who I am. Another thought I had was as long as I'm stuck and I keep looking back, God can't reveal the plans he has for me. Right now I have to learn to know him, and to love him, and to trust him before he can even allow me to do what he wants me to do. Today I dedicate myself, thank you."

3/10/01

Though my father and mother forsake me, the Lord will receive me (Psalm 27:10)

Dear God,
It's been so long since I've written here. I still want to address these entries to myself but then it would have a different focus and I don't want to go there. I only want to focus on you and what you would have me do, or just simply be.

So much has happened, as you know. This morning I forgave your child who abused me. I acknowledged him in my heart, and I ask you to press your hand upon his heart and his mind, that he may come to ask for your forgiveness through my Lord Jesus. God, it is not up to me to condemn him and I don't want to feel angry, resentful, or carry this residual fear through my relationships with people. Every time I throw up or forego eating, it's about him having power, and God, you're the only one who has power over me! Why do I put my life in his hands? This lie has gone on for too long. God, it is like death. I look at the remaining dust and ashes and I could let despair over-rule me but a new dawn has come, Lord. Please lead me away from the dust and ashes and take me to beautiful pastures that glisten with gold in the sunlight. I am safe with you, Lord. Take my hand and lead me. Help me to trust in your divinity.

3/15/01
Dear God,
Thank you for instilling the strength and courage to share you with people who DON'T believe. Lord, I felt you calling me to share with Allen. I cried when I let an opportunity pass, but God, you make everything perfect. The second opportunity proved to be the best time. No, he didn't accept Jesus, but God, I was so encouraged by how *thoughtful* he was. I could see the Holy Spirit working on him, massaging his heart. Lord, I know it's not up to me to convert him, but I truly believe he wants to believe you and in your son, Jesus. Sixty years of living his own way is a long time. God, I want him to understand that an eternity WITHOUT you is an even longer time! Oh Lord, I wish I had thought of that when he was describing how living 80 years is nothing; meaning how short time is. Lord, I told him that I know more than ever how short time is. Even young people are dying every day. You can't say that you have your whole life ahead of you.

God, sometimes I'm afraid you will take me sooner than later, that maybe you're using me for only a short time. Please take that fear away. I shouldn't be afraid anyway. I want to be with you. I think I still have things to accomplish, God, but always remind me of your will.

Counting Bones

This next entry follows a powerful prayer session with Pastor Brian. I was completely broken after succumbing an entire weekend to the snare of the eating disorder so cleverly disguised as the devil himself. It also follows one month to the day I had bravely made an oath to the church, God, and myself. Even so, it is when we make such oaths that the devil will intensify his attack to try to break our spirits. He does not want us to succeed. He despises boldness that brings glory to God. I had a powerful ally in Pastor Brian; this is truly a man of God, when he laid his hand upon my shoulder in prayer, it was as if it was God's own hand. I felt something like an electric current surge through my body; it was a hot, glowing feeling. Now, in retrospect, I can see that God was healing me in that very moment.

The Lord is my rock my fortress and my deliverer; my God is my rock, in whom I take refuge. He is my shield and the horn of my salvation, my stronghold. I call to the Lord, who is worthy of praise, and I am saved from my enemies...He reached down on high and took hold of me; he drew me out of deep waters. He rescued me from my powerful enemy, from my foes, who were too strong for me. They confronted me in the day of my disaster, but the Lord was my support. He brought me out into a spacious place; he rescued me because he delighted in me...You, O Lord, keep my lamp burning; my God turns my darkness into light. With your help I can advance against a troop, As for God, his way is perfect; the word of the Lord is flawless. (verses from Psalm 18).

3/18/01
Dear God,

Thank you God for letting me know you and for being here with me. I'm gradually building myself up again with your help. Prayer is so powerful and wonderfully healing. I felt so peaceful, and in those moments, I believed everything was going to be OK and it is! IT WILL BE.

I denounce the enemy, Lord, in Jesus' name, this battle is already won! Lord, give me my excitement, my joy, my happiness, my connection to people through you God. For as long as I live may I be joyous in each step that I take. Fill me with your grace, God. Let me be a light. Give me your strength to not look back. YOU Lord, I want to focus on YOU. You're at the end of my path. You're the goal. You're whom I want to come to. You do not play tricks, God. You don't play, "catch me if you can". No, Lord, you're here with me. Just don't let me forget that!

Interlude:
Just a few days later, March 22, 2001, marked my 30th birthday. The milestone seemed congruent with the pattern of not looking back. I could not bear the thought of one more day lost to the evil one. It was time to put on the full armor of God, to pick up all the tools God gave me to fight the devil and his accomplices (as it states in Ephesians 6: 11-18). I also had forgiven the person who had abused me, leaving no reason for me to continue the violation towards myself. However, it was still difficult to reconcile the attitudes I had towards myself. I needed to forgive myself for the damage and wasted years incurred from self-abuse. Therefore, I honored myself on this day, pledging that there was no option to look back. The door to my twenties and earlier years was now sealed shut with the key nowhere to be found. God had been waiting for this day and I'm sure the angels were singing in heaven for today I declared my abstinence from any act of starving or purging. I was giving up the only life I knew and trusting God to be the Director. As a result, I was in for an adventure, God was about to revolutionize my life.

Hmmm…What is there to write about?
4/17/01
It has been such a long time. I don't really think about writing as much but not because it's a struggle or I've lost my enthusiasm for it. In a way, it's wonderful because there's been a freedom not to write. I trust that writing will return to me and I'll return to the writing. I've been engaged in other things. I've been writing to *other* people, supporting a couple of young women in their struggles with eating disorders. Thus, I haven't been glued to the page, but I've been connected to other people, which is really all I ever wanted to have.

I love this feeling of "showing up", being present, and seeing the effect I have on people. I could not do that with the eating disorder. I was not free to delegate my energy into things and people that were of value and importance to me. As I continue to see these things develop, it gives me ammunition to keep going. I know that one day, very soon, I WILL NOT have an eating disorder. For the first time, I don't feel sad about that. It's pure joy.

It's been almost one month of no purging. I'm not afraid of the "what ifs?" (What if this isn't real? What if I fail?) anymore because I'm confident I've cut the chords that bound me.

Whenever I think about cutting back on food, I just shake my head and immediately check that thought right out of my head. I recognize that it's just a pattern and a pattern that I can break (*I can do anything in Christ who strengthens me*, Philippians 4:13). I've been having these thoughts for so long that it's going to take time to rebuke all of them. It's like fighting cancer cells. I'm giving myself chemotherapy, zapping all of the unhealthy and negative thoughts that penetrate my mind. Over time, all of the "cancer" will be gone. I'll have to keep giving myself check-ups to remain cancer-free.

I've joined the gym. I treated myself to a full body massage. I'm not going to the gym to abuse myself. I'm going to feel strong and feel my body working for me. It's about me and my body meeting for the first time, really. It's about developing a friendship and learning to listen. It's so strange how long I opposed my body and now my body is so forgiving and kind. How gently it responds! All my body ever wanted was to be loved, nurtured, and respected. It's weird looking at my body as a part of me but also as an extension of me. For so long I walked around with "chopped" body parts; my head, arms, legs, feet, hands, everything was disconnected. I felt discombobulated. Maybe a more accurate analogy is the dog forever chasing its tail, not realizing that the tail is a part of itself.

Forgiveness has played a major part in this transformation to the "other side". I forgave the person who abused me. I needed to stop the powerful "pay-off" I was getting for abusing myself. By letting the person go I no longer had reason to continue the violation towards myself. I forgave him and now I forgive myself. Excuses and regrets don't change what's done. It's just dangerous to entertain those thoughts. I don't think I had to live 15 years with an eating disorder. I also know that it could easily go on for another 5 years. Sooner or later, a decision has to be made. I did not want to waste another year of my life in the toilet.

I know now that it was always me. It was always up to me, that this freedom has always been here for the taking and all I needed was to reach out and grab it. Before, I didn't see it, and when I *could* see it, I spiraled downward. I committed the ultimate betrayal against myself. Now I'm thankful I didn't miss another opportunity to grab onto what has rightfully been mine. I could grab onto it because I finally connected and internalized the reality that I'm indeed worth claiming. I deserve to have a life of freedom. I deserve to be loved, nurtured, and respected. I deserve my lot in life. How glorious it is! How glorious God is! The blood of the Lamb, Jesus Christ, has given all of this freedom to me.

4/28/01
Dear God,

I need to stop, turn down the static, and open my ears to listen what you have to say to me. It's been explained to me that I cannot mess up your plan. Regardless of my choices, you have a plan for me.

I want you to know that I'm willing to lay my life down for you. It may not require me to be a missionary, but in small, almost unnoticeable ways. I know that I'm being a support to Megan (a young woman in my church suffering from an eating disorder). But God, I struggle with this insecurity I'm still not doing enough for you. I'm not spending enough time with you or listening.

God, I do feel that you've called for me to become a counselor, a helper of people. If I'm wrong, please let me know. I also have a great desire to publish this journal. Again, if this is misdirected, please let me know. I'm wondering how to pursue these things. How do these pursuits become less overwhelming? I know with your help, doors will open. I trust you to keep me focused, eyes in front, on the path you want me to go. God, I really don't want to take the long way or waste any time. However, even these circumstances can become a part of your plan, or may have been all along.

I know that, more than anything, all that's important to you is for me to be in a relationship with you. If I'm obedient and faithful, that pleases you much more than the actual things I do. So God, I want not to worry about what I'm doing but rather how I'm being with you. It is how I'm *being* that will lead me to do everything you ever desired for me to do and to have. I know that what pleases you will please me also. In the end, you and I have the same purpose.

A reflection on the new rhythm of my life:
5/5/01

It's a strange thing to me that I don't feel a necessary urge to write or record everything going on. I'm forcing myself, somewhat, to write now only because I don't want to "forget" the momentous things happening. It seems "before" I didn't want to forget the misery I felt. Now I don't want to forget the joy I feel, this re-birth. With the passage of time, it can become more of a second nature. Just like learning to ride a bike or drive a car; you forget how joyous and liberating it was to gain that freedom. Yet, in a lovely way, there's contentment in letting go too. It's great not to define myself in such a way. I wondered what "normal" was and if I'd ever feel that way. I think I'm getting there. I'm no longer afraid of elusiveness. I can go after anything in my life, and I mean that in a positive way.

How I feel about my body is different too. I'm no longer interested in being a stick figure. I don't want to be bony or feel bony. It's so great that what I so highly valued before, like how far my stomach could shrink below my hipbones, are falling away like shackles. I actually think that it's attractive now to have a little curve to my stomach. It's OK to have some food in there.

Eating is getting easier. I respond to my hunger. I have what I want. It's a little reticent to have this trustworthiness with my body that I've never had before. I trust that it won't make me fat. My body reciprocates that message to me.

5/10/01

Today marks seven weeks of no starving or purging. That is a testimony of God. Lord knows I've been tempted. I still am. My body feels different. I know it could be so easy to just forget about this progress, for as hard as I have worked, it could all drain away in a matter of days. I can't be "skinny" and be connected at the same time. The irony is that I'm still a skinny person, it just doesn't meet my standards for "skinny". That's something I have to accept.

Now that I have my body and mind along the same line, my focus is breaching outward. My world isn't so inclusive. I'm looking beyond to see what's in the world, what I can offer, and what the world offers me. However, there's not the goal of what I can do for this world but what I can do for God. I know God tells me not to be afraid. Why do I keep struggling with this gnawing feeling that I'm going to miss the boat somewhere? Just jump in!

Is it enough to be earnest, willing, and eager? It feels like, when you're little and being told, "wait until you're a little older" or "you'll understand when you're older". It's frustrating because I want it now. I want to understand now! I suppose I'm never going to understand how God works. It's not my place to know. I can only trust him and abide in his way. I need to wait on the Lord.

Romans 8:5- *Those who live according to the sinful nature have their minds set on what the nature desires; but those who live in accordance with the Spirit have their minds set on what the Spirit desires.*

5/11/01

It was a good feeling to share my progress with Pastor Brian. It was helpful to know that he has struggles to drink even after 23 years of abstinence. It sometimes appears for no reason at all. So, even 23 years from now, I could still be blind-sided, but what's important is not the fact the temptation has arisen, but how I react to it.

Meeting with Jo-D today capitalized on that topic. This feeling of restlessness I have is really about standing on the edge of a breakthrough. A change is about to occur and I just have to wait on God. I have to keep my eyes peeled and be ready.

Having an eating disorder doesn't allow you to be ready for a change. An eating disorder is an antidote to change.

Changing perspectives and the waiting continues:
Wait on the Lord, be of good courage, and he shall strengthen your heart; Wait, I say, on the Lord! (Psalm 27:14)

Counting Bones

5/24/01

My relationship with writing is changing. It's strange that I don't turn to my pen and paper every time I experience perplexing feelings. It was my gateway every single day; now I merely show up every couple of weeks or so, just from a sense of obligation. I still want to retain memory through writing. Everything I'm going through right now is so important and I feel somewhat pensive that I'm not getting it down on paper.

For the most part, I don't lean on writing as much because it's no longer an escape. Instead, I'm turning to people, I'm vocalizing what I previously would have written, and I'm engaging with myself and the world around me. I find myself talking out loud and that seems to reduce my anxiety. I think out loud to myself and that helps. Now that I'm not commiserating, I can now focus on people and events outside of myself.

I feel like there's a waiting period going on, that something is going to happen soon, but I don't know what it is. It's being on the brink of a major breakthrough, that I've been waiting patiently for God to reveal to me. I've been obedient in my promise not to look back. Today marks nine weeks! It sounds so short but so long. I know God can lead me now in a way that he couldn't before and it excites me. I have to trust God to work in and through me. I can never give in. I just know that I can bear it because Jesus asks me to cast my worries upon him.

Come to me all you who are weary and burdened, and I will give you rest. Take my yoke upon you and learn from me, for I am gentle and humble in heart, and you will find rest for your souls. For my yoke is easy and my burden is light (Matthew 11: 28-30).

Interlude:

On 5/27/01 I was led to speak to my church again about the miracle that was occurring in my life. I wanted to share my joy and hope with other people. These are my words:

"I don't know what to say but that's a good thing because I just think I'm waiting for God to give me the words. A few months ago, I stood here, and I revealed that I had a struggle with an eating disorder and a past trauma of sexual abuse, which contributed, to that. I think, even now, I really don't have any idea of my testimony, how it affects people; I've been told that it has been an inspiration to people, and I'm just trusting God to keep leading me. I've really wanted to share, how in the last few months, how God has affected me and had led me. I'm sort of overwhelmed by it.

I just want to say first off, that I have struggled for 15 years, off and on, could never get out of that snare. I didn't know what it took. I just have to say that on that particular day (2/18/01) God was speaking to me, and he said, 'seize this opportunity!' and I knew that if I didn't listen that I would deeply regret it. So I just listened, and I came up, and I did what he had me do. In the weeks following that, it didn't happen right away, actually a month later is when I had my 30th birthday; something transformed in me that day, and it just came to me again, that I didn't want to live another day like that. I didn't want to live in the past. I only wanted to look forward. The height of a struggle with an eating disorder IS control, and I couldn't live a double life. Either God was in control or I was in control and I couldn't have it both ways. So I was petrified to give that away,to give up the life I've always known how to live, and what I could not do for 15 years, God has taken away from me.

It *is* one day at a time and there are days where I'm white knuckling it. But in those times God has led me to- in Luke 4, it gives an example of Jesus being tempted by Satan, and I knew from that chapter that in those moments of temptation, even Jesus was tempted and he could have given in but he didn't. It's the power of the Word, that you are to remember the Word, and that is my strength. So, in those moments, I ask 'Jesus lay your hand upon me'. I also think of 'knock and Jesus will come in (Revelation 3:20)'. So I've invited Jesus every day to come with me, to sit at the table with me, to comfort me when I'm tempted. I also think of a few weeks ago, a question Pastor Brian asked, 'Do you want to be well?' and I was faced with that question, 'Do you want to be well?' You think, that's *so easy*, but it's not. It's so simplistic, but you know, if you're following God and God is calling you, there is no such thing as status quo with God. You can't be comfortable, you can't be static; God is always calling you, changing you, and molding you into what he wants you to become in the image of Christ. He also called us to be a light to the world, and so you always have to be adjusting your wattage.

Counting Bones

Before this ever happened, I couldn't understand when people would say, you know, I drank, I smoked, or I did drugs, and then I found God and that was it! What does that mean? There's so much more behind that. It is that simple and yet it's not. I'm hoping, just by sharing this testimony that...there are a few things that were entailed in that.

One was healing; you have to believe that you can be healed. I'm not for one second thinking that this struggle is over, but I do believe, that if I just believe and I continually wait upon God, that yes, I do believe in a full healing. One day all of this will fall away. The second thing was forgiveness and I never would have believed that this would happen either, but the person who abused me, I forgave. It was simple. I just realized in order not to look back, in looking back upon the abuse, that there really wasn't any more reason for me to abuse myself. And if that had never happened to me I may never have even come to know the Lord, so there was a blessing in disguise. That person, wherever he is right now, is also a child of God. He may have been abused himself, I don't know, but I pray that one day he will also come to know God. Also significant, coming right up here after prayer, I would have to say that prayer, the cell group, has been instrumental in my healing. Bill (a cell group member and also an elder of the church), I must say, your prayer certainly contributed to a breakthrough. God says that Jesus will come where two or more people are gathered. It seems my own prayers, I'm sure that my own prayers by themselves...it's like I needed the help of other people praying for me. Being in a cell group, its weekly support, but it's also seeing love in action. When you don't know how to love yourself, I would say the best way to find out is to watch other people, to see love in action. The last thing I wanted to share was the breakthrough. As I said before, when I initially came up here, that if you're always stuck in the past, you can never know what God has planned for you. I certainly never expected what God has done for me now. I trust that there is more to come. Also it's a partnership; it's discipline and dependency, you can't have one or the other. God will be God and you will be you, but he expects you to do your work and he expects you to have faith in him to do his work.

I thank you for letting me share with you today. I just want to say how much I love you, and I've appreciated your support. Thank you."

6/2/01
72 days. That's how long it's been without throwing up. It seems like an eternity. I don't even want to imagine what it would take for me to give in. I've already been tempted quite enough. What is this difference? How could something that was so hard to give up become something that is so hard to give in?

Interlude:
On 6/9/01 I was baptized! It was a very special day for me. I had sent a letter to all of my family members in New York, basically telling them everything that I had testified in church. It was the first time that I was telling them about my faith; that I had accepted Jesus Christ as my personal savior, what that meant to me, and how he was changing my life. It occurred to me to write a letter as a follow up to one I had written when I was 16 years old, disclosing my battle with an eating disorder. Who knew it would have waged on for half of my young life? It seemed like a full circle announcement. I wanted to let them know this was a permanent change. So now, when they see the difference in me, they'll know it's because of God's glory.

The baptism, by itself, would have been special enough. But God came to meet me and he revealed to me everything about myself that made it clear it was he who was speaking. He gave me a vision that was very reassuring, loving, and hopeful. Part of the message was that my testimony and my very presence, just being who I am, would lead people to God. Writing this book has been a partnership. After all, God is the author of my life.

Going the next mile with Christ:
6/26/01
Give me boldness, Lord. Let me testify to your name. People have questions, God. They have forgotten what you have- and have not- created. Your Word brings clarity. I am to read your Word to see what you say about the issue. The world

misconstrues and twists everything into their own little truth. The world has forgotten truth. They have justified sin as "just the way things are". Not true!! Lord, you are my daily bread. You are the air I breathe. Please, Lord, let me carry a torch. Let me be strong and unwavering. Help me to speak the truth. Let me be bold. My father in heaven, how I want to make you proud!

And then Satan says, "Not so fast!" A prayer of counter-attack:

Dearest God,
    You give me everything I need God to fight this war. Lord, I will not allow the evil one to plant thoughts in my head designed to destroy my mind and then my body. Even if my body were destroyed God, doesn't Satan know that I belong to you (*I have summoned you by name; you are mine.* Isaiah 43:1)? He can't win! Jesus sealed my fate on the cross (2 Corinthians 5:15). Jesus said he would never abandon me (Matthew 28: 20). He also said that I would recognize his voice and follow him (John 10: 3-4). There will always be a door to escape into his comforting arms when the temptation is too great (1 Corinthians 10:13).
    Father, I ask for trust, strength and faith. I rebuke these false truths, these thoughts that I'm fat, that I don't feel right, and it would be easier if I lost weight. I rebuke these thoughts in Jesus' name! Flee from me you devil! You cannot have me. Your plan will not work as it so often did before. I'm a different person now. I claim my heritage. I am God's daughter and I belong to him!
Thank you Jesus for saving me.
Thank you Father, for Jesus.
Together forever, Amen.

7/11/01
Dear God,
    I am still tormented by obsessive thoughts. I hate how I feel. I feel so heavy. I think I'm fat. I know it's not true logically, but it's too much for me. I want to take things into my own hands. Where are you? I don't feel your divine touch. God, I want to give in! It makes me angry. Why now? Why can't this just be lifted? Help me Jesus, to fight it off. God, I feel so demanding. I should

be praising you instead of asking, asking, asking. I don't know what else to do. Of course, right now, I don't have my Bible with me, as I should be reading your Word. I feel helpless because I am ill prepared for battle.

Lord Jesus, be with me today more urgently than ever, for I feel more fragile than you know. The fragileness> it's all in my head, I'm sure, for how can I lose with you by my side? Still, it's a comfort to call out your name, even knowing that you shall not forsake me. I don't trust my human will. I'm afraid of succumbing to weak desires. I fantasize about cutting out certain foods, exercising, "getting lean", so that I can feel in control again. I must admit this even though you already know the struggle in my head. I'm examining myself in the mirror from all angles and pinching for fat, tracing bones that no longer stick out, and I get angry and self-loathing. Why am I feeling this way when I have seen the opposite?

Lord, help me through this day. Live in me today. Guide all my actions, thoughts, and words. I pray for freedom from this obsession in the name of the one who freed me and continues to free me, ****JESUS****.

Immediately after writing this prayer, an answer came to me and it's so simple and profound. I must focus on others to get myself out of this self-absorption. I must look to God first to live my life, as he would want me to. There is a difference between self-absorption and self-awareness and it's like a seesaw. I've been self-absorbed, and as a result, feelings of anger, torment, and anguish erupted, all of which are not of God or from him (1 Corinthians 14:33). Wow. What a great insight. Thank you God for helping me see that.

Later in the day:

<u>Surviving Satan's attack:</u>
I came so close to purging today. I thought about what it would mean and how I would feel. I was at a place where I felt that I didn't care but knew it was all gut-wrenching emotion that was driving my thinking into irrationality. I had to think about what made this time different from all the other temptations I felt. What I ate wasn't out of the ordinary.

Counting Bones

It just seems to have this cumulative effect- I was thinking about what I've eaten over a string of days and the last several weeks (remember about not looking back!). My body isn't much bigger but it *feels* different. What's thin, or even considered really thin, isn't relevant to me. Anything that isn't concave to me is the equivalent of being fat.

So how did I save myself? I left a message on Jo-D's machine to confirm my resolve not to give in. I almost gave in when I called Jena and she wasn't home. Believe it or not, I ended up in a bathroom stall, but I used its privacy as a sanctuary rather than an outlet of self-destruction. I started breathing in and out while I prayed at the same time. With arms outstretched, I kept calling out to Jesus knowing that the power of his name would drive the devil away. Within a couple minutes I felt ready to face the world. I had my composure again.

The main reason, I thought of not to purge, was that I knew it would change my life forever. That sounds really dramatic but I couldn't take that risk. I just know that one act of compulsion and impulse would start a chain reaction, that maybe I would never regain what I've accomplished. And there's also the real danger of hurting myself permanently. Purging now could pose greater physical risk after having abstained for months. I can't guarantee that my body wouldn't have an alarming reaction. There's always the chance that "this time" could kill me.

7/13/01

But, wait, Satan's not through with me yet! However, God does prevail, and a miraculous breakthrough occurs:

Thank you God for beckoning me to spend time with you. I've been so perplexed by the torment I've been feeling. Yet again, I was so tempted to purge. It was so familiar; I could have done it without thinking. And instead of cramming my mind with other stimuli, I sat down with you. You listened. We danced, held hands, and clapped. It was so much fun!

It's amazing how quickly joy can melt into sorrow. God, I was able to cry with you, and you comforted me. I don't understand the trials again, but what I heard, is that these trials allow me to come to you (John 16:33, 2 Corinthians 4:8-9, 1 Peter

4:12). As I cried, I realized that in itself, was a miracle. I wasn't purging! I couldn't come to you when I was immersed in the eating disorder. You chose me God! You chose to heal me. You chose me to bear these trials so that I could witness to your glory. I cry with joy now. I accept these trials now God, unto your holy name.
You create me anew.
Forever you & me, Amen!

And still, Satan does not give up:
7/15/01
It's still so hard God. I think about what I'm "doing" to myself now. I feel anger and remorse that I'm eating and eating without purging. My mind taunts me that I could still go back, I can erase all the feelings of discomfort; it's really alluring but it's like a smoke screen. As soon as I walk through it, I'll see the demonic force for what it is. I already know now, that demons are working on my mind. Satan doesn't want me to go forward because he's afraid of my strength. He doesn't want me to win this battle.

Dear God, I guess what has made this difficult is my denial of the trials (John 10:10). For a while there, I was comfortable. But I can see now that during that stable time I was building a foundation so that I would not be knocked off my feet so that Satan could devour me.

I feel so humble to think of such company as Job, Joseph, and Paul. Each of them had trials and each of them remained fastened and committed to you.

I still don't understand God, but I don't have to understand. All I have to do is just stand and keep my focus on you. I'll do what you ask me and you'll take care of the rest. I guess I lend to my own torment, thinking there's something more I should be doing or not doing, in this battle. On the other hand, I don't want to shoot three arrows when you want me to shoot six (2 Kings 13:18-19).

Lord, spending time with you has been so special. I have felt so loved, caressed, and cherished. Even though I've been in pain, I'm thankful for it, because it drew me closer to you. There will be better times, God, and it will be so sweet, because I

endured it and claimed victory through Jesus' name. Jesus lives in me. Glory be to God.
Rejoice in the Lord always. I will say it again: Rejoice! Let your gentleness be evident to all. The Lord is near. Do not be anxious about anything, but in everything, by prayer and petition, with thanksgiving, present your requests to God, which transcends all understanding, will guard your hearts and your minds in Christ Jesus.

Finally, brothers, whatever is true, whatever is noble, whatever is pure, whatever is lovely, whatever is admirable- if anything is excellent or praiseworthy- think about such things. Whatever you have learned or received or heard from me, or seen in me- put it into practice. And the God of peace will be with you.
(Philippians 4:4-9)

EPILOGUE

As I write this, it is in the midst of the joy, wonder, and expectation of the Christmas season as the world commemorates the birthday of our Lord Jesus Christ. After a long journey of waiting, I feel the same sentiment with the birthing of this book. I anticipate with great joy the miracles God is going to do in the healing and deliverance of His people. I am deeply humbled and honored that God would choose me to be His vessel to accomplish His work. God does work all things for good for those who love Him and according to His purpose.

I know there will be a curiosity in how I'm doing now. It is still a process for me. Although I do not actively engage in eating disorder behaviors, it's still a process of disentangling myself from old mindsets. Often times when there is victory, Satan will use any opportunity to punch our weak spots. Moreover, he has a sly way of making our *feelings* appear as reality. However, the Word of God says that all old things have passed away and we are created new in Christ Jesus! Praise God that He is strong when we are weak!

For a long time I believed a lie that Satan fed to me. I thought that as long as I struggled with temptation and the after effects of an eating disorder that it would disqualify my testimony. I learned in God's grace, that nothing could be further from the truth. God says what disqualifies me qualifies me. The apostle Paul prayed to God three times for the persistent thorn in his side to be removed. God's response was, "My grace is sufficient for you." I have claimed that promise for myself. By walking through this journey I will only have more compassion for people who endure this same struggle.

It is important to understand that merely breaking the cycle of starvation, binging, and purging was just the beginning of breaking strongholds. I have created a new definition for an eating disorder and it's a spiritual warfare designed to destroy the mind and then the body. It wasn't what I was doing to my body that was life threatening; it was the war going on inside my mind that was attacking my body. That's why it is so vital to renew your mind daily so that you can be fit against the wiles of the devil.

Counting Bones

Over time, God has been delivering me from glory to glory. What the world says would have taken years to recover, or even a hopeless case, God has transformed for His glory. This makes Satan very angry. This book is quite destructive to his kingdom. I find it extremely gratifying to uncover the gimmicks and tricks the devil uses to scheme and deceive, and expose him! In order to see the truth, the whole truth, you have to be willing to break those strongholds.

Perhaps the biggest stronghold was breaking the scale I owned. Instead of measuring myself by numbers, I now completely look to God. I look up to heaven. When I shattered that stronghold (I smashed it to the ground. When it hit the ground, something supernatural occurred. I felt my life speed up by ten paces. Whatever had been hindered could now move through), an immediate revelation poured into me.

We all come in different sizes and shapes and yet none of it was a mistake. We are perfectly designed in His love and image. Who are we to criticize and judge His work? I consider all the anorexics, bulimics, and women who generally try to conform to this ONE image and it's a big, fat lie! When you take it at face level, you can see how simple and absurd it is. Satan takes his time in forming a lie, for if he tried to tell us all at once, we would never fall for it. Honestly, doesn't it seem stupid for everyone to look and sound alike? Yet, isn't this exactly what we're seeing taking place in the world? Millions of people are falling into this deceptive trap. That is what the world is coming to- everything is being narrowed down into one order- one money system, one government, one code, etc. Thus it seems interesting that there's an obsession with numbers in this country and even around the world.

We are obsessed with calories, weight, clothing size, bank accounts, stocks; external things to keep us distracted from internal truth. In the end, people are going to be convinced that they have to take the mark, a number that will strip away all identity. It's all very subtle and seductive. Satan convinces the anorexic that her weight is her identity. Very cunning, isn't it?

So what then, do we hold fast to? God's promises and words last for all eternity. When he speaks, His word does not return void. Your truth is what God says you are: a conqueror, a

Michelle Bahret

victor, precious, gentle, pure, and righteous. When you feel fragile, meek, and delicate run to the Lord for refuge and He will be your strength. Don't believe in the cunning whispers of the devil. Believe in God's word, for He is your foundation, your rock, and your deliverer. His word is the same as yesterday, today, and forevermore. Trust Him! He is the Way. He is the Life. He knew you before you were born. He knitted you in your mother's womb. Don't you think his creation is perfect? The battle for perfection wears on in this fallen world, but take heart, for perfection has come and this perfection lives inside of you: the beautiful and radiant spirit of your Lord Jesus Christ.

In closing, this scripture says it all, Now *the Lord is the Spirit, and where the Spirit of the Lord is, there is Freedom* (2 Corinthians 3:17)! I am free, healed, and delivered in the name of Jesus Christ, Amen! God bless you my friend. Thank you for sharing this journey with me.

Michelle Bahret
December 2002

Printed in the United States
15862LVS00004B/79-102